'You ladies out there who may have a blemished love life might find it as amusing as I did' – Lisa Marie Presley

'The authors offer firmly tongue-in-cheek characterizations of men, organized by sign, for the date-weary hetero woman' – *Publishers Weekly*

'Valentine void? No romance? Grab a mope-busting new read' – *Glamour* (USA)

'Think of it as a salve for the heartbroken female on Valentine's Day' – *Milwaukee Journal-Sentinel*

'With so many astro-tomes weighted down by portentousness and a desire to be scrupulously even-handed when presenting the attributes of the 12 signs, a wildly prejudiced account of the zodiac is refreshing' – *The Observer*

'Totally subjective and unashamedly sexist, it takes each star sign in turn and tells you exactly why they are the enemy' – *The Guardian*

D0795294

'Whether the bloke is an ignorant know-it-all, or a highly-strung deviant, it's down to his star sign, according to a new book, *How to Spot a B*stard by His Star Sign . . .*' – *Daily Mirror*

'It'll certainly have you looking to the heavens in despair, girls' – *The Sun*

'Dip into this madcap stocking filler . . . and laugh and sneer your broken heart away' – *Company*

'If you love Gloria Gaynor's hit "I Will Survive" this is your ultimate horoscope book' – *Bristol Evening Post*

'Great fun and well written' – *Paisley Daily Express*

'This is the horoscope that goes where no other has ever gone before' – *Sunday Mail* (Glasgow)

'A terrific little book' – *Aberdeen Evening Express*

'Now you won't have to wade your way through a load of Mr Wrongs' – *Chat*

HOW TO
SPOT A
B*STARD
BY HIS STAR SIGN

▶ *Adèle Lang & Susi Rajah*

MAINSTREAM
PUBLISHING
EDINBURGH AND LONDON

This edition 2004

Copyright © Adèle Lang and Susi Rajah, 1996, 2001

First published in Great Britain by
MAINSTREAM PUBLISHING COMPANY (EDINBURGH) LTD
7 Albany Street
Edinburgh EH1 3UG

First published in 1996 in Australia by Pan Macmillan Australia Pty Limited
Revised edition published in 2001 by Pan Macmillan

ISBN 1 84018 860 X

Reprinted 2004 (twice)

A catalogue record for this book is available from the British Library

Typeset in Futura and Garamond
Printed and bound in Great Britain by
Bookmarque Limited, Croydon, Surrey

The authors of this book have been using astrology to prejudge and persecute men for years. Both being fire signs, they're always right and never wrong. *How to Spot a B*stard by his Star Sign* has been used against men in eleven countries to date.

Adèle Lang and Susi Rajah are also the authors of *I'm Not a Feminist, But . . .* which has recently been published in the USA.

As well as being the resident astrologer for *Heat*, *Marie Claire* and *J17* magazines in the UK, Adèle is the author of the *New York Times* best-selling *Confessions of a Sociopathic Social Climber*. She lives in Bristol with a Taurus bastard.

Susi is working on her first novel. She lives in LA with a Gemini bastard.

**To Jonny Abba and Corey Mitchell –
the nicest bastards we know.**

Acknowledgements

Our gratitude to: Jane Burridge and Alison Urquhart who found a UK home for this book after its Antipodean birth; Anne Dewe for continuing to conquer the European Union and Carin Siegfried for steering us towards world domination via the States; Fiona Brownlee for being the best walking advertisement an author could have; and Bill Campbell and Peter MacKenzie for seeing the book's ongoing potential in spite of being men.

Adèle Lang & Susi Rajah

Contents

NEW! Compatibility Tests
Which Bastard Are *You* Compatible With? 115

How *do* you spot a bastard
by his star sign?

Some men might seem like natural-born bastards. Others will appear to have grown into the role over a period of time and a life of hard knocks. Don't be fooled. So far as men and their less appealing characteristics go, genetic make-up and social conditioning have got absolutely nothing to do with it. Put simply, all men are bastards by dint of their star signs.

It might be the disgraceful state of their attire. It might be the abysmal state of their bank accounts. It might even be their very questionable states of mind. Whatever. This guide will show you how to spot and get rid of each and every one of these astrological losers, without the use of telescopes or telescopic rifles.

Of course, what you choose to do with the information at hand is entirely up to you. The hard-core man-hating element amongst you will no doubt use it to embarrass, emasculate and/or shoot any guy who dares to come near you. The middle-of-the-road majority will pick and choose which male-baiting snippets to believe depending upon who you love or loathe at the time. And the utterly hopeless romantics in our midst will ignore our advice completely because, after all, your future unhappiness depends upon it.

Last but not least, those few-and-far-between male readers out there will probably deem our findings to be pure cod-psychology and pseudo-scientific mumbo jumbo. Well, tough. We prefer to term it 'painstaking, self-sacrificing and bone-cringingly honest research conducted over a number of years with a number of bastards for the benefit of women everywhere'.

We're-Hot-So-Shut-Up-And-Worship-Us

FIRE SIGNS

Aries ★ Leo ★ Sagittarius

Out-of-control control freaks. Untalented show-offs. Pig-ignorant know-it-alls. And that's their good points. These self-proclaimed demi-gods will try to get your attention at the merest hint of provocation (e.g. you happen to be in the same room as them).

Fire Sign bastards are always better than you and will never fail to tell you so. They'll then hammer the fact home by telling you again – just in case you didn't hear them the first time.

Dare to disagree and they'll act in their usual endearing way. They'll start yelling, turn puce and then hurl themselves to the ground with much thrashing about of arms and legs. Five minutes later they'll get back up again and act as if nothing's happened. Real astrologers like to call this their 'quick temperedness'. We like to call men in white coats.

Of course, you could choose to ignore Fire Sign bastards and hope they'll just go away. Like, right. Why go off and voluntarily die when they can be humoured one-thousand-four-hundred and forty-four minutes a day?

However, if the thought of kneeling at their feet in mock wonder does make you want to throw up, don't worry. You won't have to do it for long. Fire Sign bastards are such temperamental, competitive sons of bastards, they usually die early of heart attacks.

The Aries Bastard
MARCH 21–APRIL 20

ONCE UPON A TIME, IN THE DARK AGES, THERE was this quaint little term known as a *man's man*. Nobody knew quite what it meant. Except the poor unfortunate thing who was the *man's man's woman* – and she died a horrible death when she wilfully stuck her head in the oven unto which she was chained.

Then comes more enlightened times and in minces the Sensitive New Age Feeling Fellow. All of a sudden, a man's man surely must mean a gentleman of the pink persuasion and, gee, don't those scented candles look too, too, utterly utterly?

Meanwhile, back at the camp, deep in the woods, a solitary male is yelling at the top of his lungs, beating a tom-tom and sticking pins into a blow-up doll that looks a lot like Germaine Greer. This sad, lost soul is the Aries bloke. Bewildered by beauty myths, dumbfounded by daycare centres and completely baffled by consensual sex, he holds on to his masculinity as tightly as he holds on to his manhood (which is throbbing if you must know). Boy, does he yearn for the times when men were men and women were grateful.

Being the only man's man left in existence, it's lonely for him at the bottom of the food chain – even amoebas, given the chance, opt to mate with themselves.

And thank bloody Christ for that. Aries is such a chauvinist he'd root for truffles if he knew what truffles actually were. He's exactly the type of guy who thinks any man who buys scented candles is a raving poofter.

So, if the bastard you fancy puts on Vivaldi in the evening, whips up a nice little *soufflé a deux* and then settles down to read Jane Austen to you, he's almost certainly gay and he's definitely not Aries. Because even an Aries fairy would be down the local hellfire club, dressed to the cat-o'-nines and slugging back Frangelico with his like-minded friends.

All Aries men enjoy hanging out at the pub with their mates. And even the dead-straight homophobic one doesn't think twice about getting sentimental with them when he's pissed. In fact, you'll swear he must be an open-and-shut closet case since he spends far more time hugging and kissing other blokes than he ever does you.

The real reason this revolting creature prefers the

company of men is because he has no choice. No right-thinking woman with two opposable thumbs and lack of tail can bear the thought of being in the same room at the same time as him. He exudes so much testosterone that not only will the fine hairs on the nape of her neck stand up, they'll actually go through a rapid growth spurt.

If you are unfortunate enough to be stuck in an enclosed space with Aries, it's best just to smile as vacuously as you can and nod your head at appropriate intervals – because you won't understand a single word he's saying. English is his second language, grunting is his first. And all he can grunt about is himself, his career, his sporting achievements and how feminists would be a lot less uptight if he gave them all a good shag.

Of course, *good* and *shag* are polar opposites when it comes to this rock-throwing Romeo. One night with Aries is enough to get thee, Linda Lovelace, to the nunnery. To put it as delicately as we can, let's just say that you won't actually have *time* to lie back and think of England.

Despite his obvious lack of sexual stamina, the Aries bastard feels biologically compelled to pursue any number of luckless ladies with a vengeance verging on primeval. His courting tactics are as subtle as a sledgehammer and not half as useful. So for God's sake, don't play hard to get. It'll only encourage him.

He'll use gorilla tactics to win you over. And why

shouldn't you be flattered to be woken at three in the morning to see his great hairy face leering through your fifth-floor bedroom window? Especially when you're entertaining a guest who just so happens to be male, totally hetero and sensitive to boot.

Said guest is likely to be kicked by said boot out of aforementioned window (which is closed). Walls will be perforated, furniture dismantled and sincere apologies extracted from you who are, by now, a sobbing heap in the corner putting the women's movement back centuries.

As he's just proven, and which he'll take great pains to point out, he's not in the least bit jealous or possessive. It's just that he likes the idea of loyalty and faithfulness. From you, that is. He'll stay faithful for as long as you stay perfect. Which you're not. Which he'll tell you. Ad nauseam. (Little known fact here: not only is the Aries bastard God's gift to women, he actually is God. And we all know what happens to those who don't believe in God. However, a few years with Aries and hell will suddenly seem like a really inviting option.) If you want to know your hair is a mess, you can't drive your car for shit and you could do with a self-help course, then you can't go wrong with Aries.

Funnily enough, it's not the same the other way around. This hypocritical oaf is quite capable of pointing out your dimply thighs without giving so much as a thought to his own disgusting flab. Don't bother picking him up on this, though – the subtleties of irony will be lost in translation.

So, if you like being told what to do, how to do it and when to do it, this one's for you. If you have a mind of your own and occasionally like to use it, tell him to get lost. But put the kettle on and warm his slippers before you go.

If you do decide to leave, don't expect him to take it lying down. Lying down is your job. In the game of life, the term 'gracious in defeat' is hard enough for Aries to pronounce, let alone practise. Beat him at something as trivial as Scrabble and he'll proclaim – once he's started speaking to you again – that Scrabble is a game of luck, requires absolutely no intelligence and, besides, you got all the As, Bs and Cs and he got all the Qs, Xs and Zs and no vowels whatsoever.

Of course, no matter which way you play it you can't win. Because he's even more unbearable on the extremely rare occasion he does manage to outwit you. He'll crow that Scrabble is a game of skill and bang on about how he managed to make really big words like CAT out of very hard letters like C, A and T. (Note: If he does attempt to be humble in victory, he's just fishing for compliments. Don't give him any.)

Since Aries can't cope with you beating him at a board game, it therefore follows he'll be positively suicidal if you outdo him in the boardroom. So quit before you get ahead. Because if you do start scoring more fame, fortune and frequent flier points than him, he'll just try and get you pregnant.

How to spot one

Throw peanuts. If he catches them in his mouth, he's probably Aries. And if he then starts beating his chest and picking lint off your clothes, he's definitely Aries.

Where to find one

Commandeering a cave. Moving his lips whilst reading *The Cat in the Hat*. Or marching at a Real Men Against Women's Rights To Answer Back rally. If he's in the kitchen, he's obviously lost.

How to intrigue one

This is tricky because you need to be two things at once. You've got to be loud and obnoxious so he thinks he's found his soul mate. At the same time you must show your soft, feminine side so his masculinity isn't threatened. The best way to do both simultaneously is to hurl spitballs at the pavement whilst taking care not to hit your Laura Ashley frock.

The first date

He'll either take you to the zoo to meet his family or else he'll invite you to the annual Especially Privileged

Ladies' Night at the Masonic Lodge and tell you what you'd like to eat, how much you'd like to drink and be horrified when you attempt to open your mouth for anything other than eating.

When to do the deed

Whenever. If he doesn't have honourable intentions, he'll think you're a slut but have sex with you anyway. If he does like you, he'll still have sex with you and then wake you to propose.

When to pop the question

Don't. That's the man's job. Just relax and enjoy your independence whilst you still have it. You'll have years to regret giving it up.

If he dumps you

Forget him. Since the Aries bastard is incapable of admitting he's wrong – particularly in front of a woman – he's hardly likely to come loping back into your life declaring it was all a big mistake. If he does, it's only because no other woman will have him.

If you dump him

He'll chase you because it won't occur to him that you can ignore his sheer animal magnetism. Keep running. He'll trip over his knuckles sooner or later.

The Leo Bastard
JULY 24–AUGUST 23

Introductory note

IT MUST BE POINTED OUT THAT MR LEO'S PLAY IS yet to be performed in a real theatre. But we are informed by Mr Leo this is due to protracted negotiations with producers in London who are terribly anxious to buy the rights – as Mr Leo himself said – this play has 'Broadway' written all over it. And even taking into account this is the first play Mr Leo has penned – in fact, his first piece of creative writing since high school – we have to say (*because he is forcing us to*), he is an outstanding master of the genre. This is a model modern short play. It displays an art of construction one usually only expects from the most revered and respected of writers. (*Is that enough?*) His dialogue, too, is worthy of much praise. Its deftness defies description; it never halts; it moves from beginning to end without a dull moment. And it's so amazingly true to life. Except wittier. And sharper. And more poignant. Its sheer brilliance will astound you and leave you gasping for more. (*There, satisfied now?*) We truly appreciate Mr Leo's generosity in allowing us to print his amazing, soon-to-be-much-lauded play in this most unworthy tome.

THE LOVES OF LEO

Written by Leo. Produced by Leo. Directed by Leo. Starring Leo.

Important: No performance of this play may be given unless written permission has been obtained from Leo and he is allowed to produce, direct and star in it.

Cast of Characters

Leo, played by himself. (*The unbelievably dashing, irresistible, courageous – not to mention terrifically handsome – hero of the play, around whom all the action revolves.*)

The Beautiful Heroine, played by you. (*Minor though important supporting role.*)

The Beautiful-Heroine's-More-Beautiful Rival, in this instance played by Catherine Zeta-Jones. (*This is the role every other woman on earth is vying for. The purpose of this character is to make the heroine realise just what she is up against and to make her suitably grateful when Leo finally chooses her.*)

The Much-Less-Exciting Man, played by someone like Brad Pitt. (*This role is really just that of an extra – a clever plot device to point out how inferior all other men are to Leo. Naturally, there is no chance of the heroine or any other woman in the world preferring this lesser man to Leo.*)

The Beautiful Maid, played by you. (*Again, another minor though important supporting role.*)

The Very Appreciative Audience, played by you, Catherine Zeta-Jones and all the other women in the world.

NB: All the characters are in modern costume. Leo is wearing faultless, immaculately tailored evening clothes which set off his hair, height and colouring perfectly. As for the rest of the cast, well, it doesn't really matter what they're wearing, does it?

Act One

Scene: The tastefully and delightfully appointed drawing-room of Leo's house. The Beautiful Heroine, The Beautiful-Heroine's-More-Beautiful Rival and The Much-Less-Exciting Man are all present and seated. [*The Very Appreciative Audience is also present but not visible.*] There is an air of melancholy about the three as they are all desperately missing the sparkling presence of their charming host who has momentarily left the room. After a couple of suspense-filled minutes, the drawing-room doors are flung open with a flourish and Leo enters, causing the whole room to look brighter as a result of his charming, sparkling presence.

Leo [*looking around*]: Hello, everybody. Why so glum? Have you been missing the sparkling presence of your charming host? [*The Very Appreciative Audience bursts into wild applause, making it impossible for the play to continue for about five minutes.*]

Leo [*starting to speak amid the subsiding applause, longing sighs and occasional fainting of The Very Appreciative Audience – showing all the world he is not the egotist he is wrongfully reported to be*]: Well? [*Once again, Leo shows why he is regarded as the saviour of the lost art of drawing room conversation.*]

The Beautiful Heroine and the Beautiful-Heroine's-More-Beautiful Rival [*in unison whilst gazing adoringly at Leo – as one does*]: Yes, we missed you terribly. Life is not the same without you.

Leo [*brushing off this blatant but understandable adoration*]: How about a drink, then? Where is that maid of mine? [*Spotting The Beautiful Heroine*] Get us all a drink will you, love? [*The Beautiful Heroine/Maid scurries off to do as she has been asked, grateful to be of use to her – and everybody else's – hero.*]

The Much-Less-Exciting Man [*opens his mouth to say something*]: Um . . . [*He realises just in time he can never say anything to compare to the witty, intelligent* conversation of Leo and politely leaves the room in recognition of the other man's natural superiority.]

Leo: Rather flighty chap, isn't he? [*allowing us a glimpse of the true understanding of human nature present in this exceptional man. Indeed, it causes much murmuring in The Very Appreciative Audience. At this point, The Beautiful Heroine returns to the room with drinks for everyone. Neither she nor The Beautiful-Heroine's-More-Beautiful Rival even notices The Much-Less-Exciting Man has left. It is difficult for them to notice anyone else when Leo is in the room.*]

Leo [*taking a drink and a handful of the delicate, mouth-watering pastries The Beautiful Heroine whipped up whilst she was fetching the drinks*]: Hey, these are good. [*The Very Appreciative Audience spontaneously bursts into thunderous cheering at this heartfelt compliment to The Beautiful Heroine because it indicates Leo knows women like it when you say nice stuff to them and also shows he is not swayed by mere physical beauty. After all, The Beautiful-Heroine's-More-Beautiful Rival is better looking but Leo never said anything to her.*]

Leo [*playing to the audience*]: Yes. [*nods, causing himself to look even more thoughtful and handsome*] Very good indeed. [*The Very Appreciative Audience erupts once more and The Beautiful-Heroine's-More-Beautiful Rival dashes off to the kitchen in an attempt to gain Leo's attention.*]

Leo [*to The Beautiful Heroine, demonstrating his awesome powers of observation*]: It looks like we're alone.
   Curtain
[*The Very Appreciative Audience leaps to its collective feet to give a two-hour standing ovation to the genius responsible for the play.*]

Concluding note

Once again, Mr Leo has requested we point out the brilliance of his play, this time by focusing on the gargantuan intellect it must have taken to produce the cliffhanger ending. Naturally, he won't leave you in suspense forever and we're sure you'll all await the sequel with bated breath. He's going to call it *The Loves of Leo II: To Be Or Not To Be*. (*Okay, look, you tell him it's been done before. We've had it.*)

How to spot one

His entrance will always be preceded by a drum roll. If you miss his entrance you'll find him already strategically positioned under a spotlight. You can't miss him there – not with the two game show hostesses on either side of him pointing him out. You might also notice The Hand Of God above his head scrawling a cloudy message in the air: women of the world, my gift to you. Regards, God. PS: Those of you who don't believe in me can also have him.

Where to find one

Anywhere there is an audience of at least one.

How to intrigue one

Look up at him in awe and wonder and say ingenuously: 'My, what a big, strong man you are', 'Gee, I wish I were as smart/witty/brave as you' or 'Are you a famous movie star?' Or just wear a full-length mirror around your neck and don't say anything at all.

The first date

The first date will be quite enjoyable. You won't have heard all his stories about himself before so you'll find them quite entertaining. They're even bearable when you hear them for the second time on your second date.

When to do the deed

On the third date. You need to do something to avoid hearing his life story again and sex will shut him up nicely. Of course, earplugs or refusing to see him any more would have the same effect but we're working under the same assumption he is – that, in the course of two dates, you will have fallen madly in love with him and now find it impossible to live without him.

When to pop the question

He'll decide when you want to get married. Just be ready to answer with a breathless 'Yes, of course' when he lets you know where and when the wedding's taking place. Then pretend your tears are tears of joy when he shows you the lace monstrosity you'll be wearing. And appear to be suitably grateful when he informs you you're allowed to choose one bridesmaid to go with the six he's already selected.

If he dumps you

Did you dare to leave your much-sought-after position at his feet being adoring in order to go to work? Did you exchange entire sentences with another man (never mind that he was your brother-in-law)? Did you have a point of view other than his? Or did you laugh at him when he wasn't being intentionally funny? Well, then, we're not surprised. You had it coming to you.

If you dump him

That you'd want to do this is completely beyond the realms of possibility.

The Sagittarius Bastard
NOVEMBER 23–DECEMBER 21

PS: SAGITTARIUS DOES EVERYTHING BACK TO front. He speaks before he thinks, leaps before he looks and loves you only after you've left him. Which is why when people say Sagittarius is a lucky bastard, they're dead right. The fact you haven't murdered him yet is a miracle. The fact his other girlfriends haven't either is a godsend. The fact real astrologers can find pleasant things to say about him, wasting entire virgin rainforests in the process, is pure magic.

In the olden days, philosophers used to comfort themselves with the knowledge that: 'I think, therefore I am not Sagittarius.' No small thanks to time and a proliferation of Piscean protest groups who didn't like victimisation of any kind unless it was specifically directed at them, the phrase became bastardised somewhat and now Sagittarius still wouldn't have a clue what it meant.

What the wise old men of yore were trying to say, no doubt, is that the Sagittarius bastard dives head first into mind-bogglingly unsuitable situations without so much as a second thought, because first ones are hard enough.

Then, when what men and women of science kindly refer to as his 'brain' has had time to catch up with his actions, he jumps back out again just as quickly. (In a perfect world, a man who acted on impulse would be forced by your enraged, shotgun-wielding father to live with, pay for and, indeed, *marry* his mistake. This, however, is the real world, and in the real world you've got Sagittarius running amok getting young girls pregnant and then leaving them for other young girls he can get pregnant, with nary a wistful glance backwards nor a bullet to the head.)

More irritating than the cold sores you'll mysteriously begin to develop, is the fact that Sagittarius is the one who started it all in the first place by hurling himself at your feet, literally begging to be enslaved. But as soon as you experience that warm fuzzy feeling in the pit of your stomach commonly known as love/ulcer/morning sickness, he's up and off.

It's not because you aren't the love of his life – don't

get him wrong. It's just that now he's had time to think (*sic*) about it, he's finally realised current relationship problems could be due to the fact you're a black, radical feminist-communist whose favourite pastime is abseiling and he's a white, moderate chauvinist-fascist who's terrified of scaling great heights.

The Sagittarius bastard's blind refusal to contemplate foresight before hindsight could be excused (because by now you'll have realised what you aren't missing) if at the same time he didn't have the temerity to tell you it was all *your* fault and that you tricked him into it.

You didn't *tell* him you were black. And why *shouldn't* he think the extremely rare and valuable lithograph of Joseph Stalin above your mantelpiece was a portrait of your dad? And how was *he* to know you were a diehard feminist? You cooked dinner for him once, *didn't* you? Okay, yes, he did have to pick your underarm hairs out of the pasta, but *so*?

Frankly, it just serves as a good excuse for him to be as unfaithful as he likes without all the boring guilt that goes along with it.

To say Sagittarius has a deep-rooted fear of monogamy is to say Salman Rushdie is slightly perturbed about dying. Indeed, advertising wankers have been able to retire on the government proceeds they received for the rash of safe sex campaigns created especially for all the Sagittarius bastard's girlfriends.

(The original slogan: 'Avoid Sagittarius like the plague, otherwise you'll end up catching it' was ditched during research when the male Scorpio component complained about out-and-out favouritism.)

Sagittarius doesn't own a stereo, not because he can't afford one (which he can't) but because the word hi-fidelity sends him into a cold sweat as opposed to the hot one he got after the last dose of herpes.

Truth be said, though, the Sagittarius bastard's honesty is something to behold. If he's screwed around he'll tell you. In excruciating detail. When you gently hint you don't care to know who put whose hand where, he'll put his great big foot in his great big mouth and tell you that, well, actually, come to not think about it, it wasn't actually a hand, it was . . . (at this stage, you are fully within your rights to put your hand, which is clenched, into his mouth, which is open, and fill it full of loose teeth).

If and when you meet his family, you'll notice they too are hideously embarrassed by his tactless words and thoughtless manner. You'll soon appreciate why he was kicked out of home at an early age and is only ever allowed back for major family get-togethers. Like funerals. And even then, in others' darkest hours, he still can't help but dig himself into a very large hole.

Asking his sister where her husband is (he's the one in the coffin) is a good example of one of his more minor gaffes. In a hurried attempt to make amends, he'll tell her he was only joking. When she promptly bursts into tears, he'll try and make her feel better by saying he didn't think she and her now-dead spouse were all that well suited anyway.

If the monumental blunders weren't bad enough, there's always the obligatory Sagittarius bluster to make you wish the ground would open up and swallow him. Since he doesn't have two IQ points to rub together, Sagittarius doesn't actually *realise* he's an intellectual dwarf. So, at the wake, this walking claptrap will regale you and his relatives with facts about which he knows absolutely nothing – completely oblivious to the fact that the lot of you are pointedly snoring. Ancient embalming techniques, Celtic burial rites and the psychological effects of reincarnation upon loopy Hollywood actresses – you name it, Sagittarius will be able to prattle on without a pause.

Take him to task about his source and he'll say he read it in a book. Since you know he doesn't read anything he hasn't written himself and you just *know* he can't write because you do his remedial English assignments for him, you'll feel compelled to point out to him that *Playboy* doesn't count. Any rare pearls of wisdom which do accidentally stream from his lips are usually poached from someone who's more intellectually gifted. Like you, for example.

Which brings us to our next point. If you're so smart, what the hell are you doing dating him? And don't start telling us it's because he's *generous*.

Yes, Sagittarius might scatter money around as profligately as his seed. But this isn't generosity, this is fiscal promiscuity. Once he's spent all his money and his family's money, he'll start spending yours. When that runs out he'll proceed to spend the earnings of his other girlfriends. Then the bank's. Then the credit union's. And then the loan shark's.

Again, it won't be his fault when he's eventually had up for bankruptcy/embezzlement/fraud in a High Court or else found in some squalid bedsit sharing pillows with a horse's head. Why didn't you *tell* him those things with all the columns of numbers were loan default statements? How was *he* to know the anonymous letters featuring clipped-out-of-newspaper words like PAY, UP, OR, YOU and DIE were death threats? Anyway, what are you doing still hanging around? Didn't he *leave* you? And don't say you're still with him because he's a bloody lucky bastard. He *knows* that. What d'you think he is? *Stupid*?

How to spot one

He's usually long of limb and short of cash. The wandering eye is not an optical dysfunction, no matter how many times he tries to convince you otherwise.

Where to find one

In a flotation tank clearing his head. In a think-tank feeling out of his depth. At a bank asking for credit. At a brothel making a deposit.

How to intrigue one

Act intelligent.

The first date

If he thinks he can get you into bed, expect to be lavished. Just don't be surprised when the debt collectors arrive at the restaurant to take away your meal.

When to do the deed

Do so at your own risk. If you start developing facial lesions and can't shake that particularly nasty bout of pneumonia, seek medical advice immediately.

When to pop the question

When you decide you'd like to be a divorcee in the not-too-distant future.

If he dumps you

Count yourself lucky but feign devastation nonetheless. And make sure he pays you the money he owes you.

If you dump him

It'll take some time for the words to sink in. So start day one with 'You're', day two with 'dumped' and on day three really put the knife in with 'thicko'.

Hi-We're-The-Most-Boring-Men-On

EARTH SIGNS

TAURUS ★ VIRGO ★ CAPRICORN

'Safe, solid and reliable' can be used to describe a very large bank. Or a bloody boring man.

Earth Sign bastards are the astrological nice guys. That's not a horrible thing to say? Okay, recall the last time a man was bowled over when you told him he was 'a really nice guy but . . .'? Who wants to date someone only your mother could love?

Of course, she'll adore the fact your Earth Sign bastard boyfriends can remember the birthdays of all her grandchildren and can name every single one of the forty thousand varieties of flora and fauna in her backyard – *in Latin*.

Your dad will be similarly impressed by your Earth Sign bastard boyfriends' ability to fill in tax forms properly, as well as their distinct inability to have dishonourable intentions towards his daughter.

Seriously, though, if you do want to wear unflattering white for a day, experience agonising labour pains and take on a crippling mortgage, then snag one of these bastards. They're so determined to do everything by rote, marriage with them really will appear to last for ever and ever.

Because they never take exciting risks or indulge in fun-fun-fun vices, Earth Sign bastards live long and healthy lives. With a bit of luck, though, they'll bore you to death. Preferably sooner rather than later.

The Taurus Bastard
APRIL 21–MAY 21

YOU'RE WEANING YOURSELF OFF THE LITHIUM AND you're in the process of finding a new job, savings account and country to live in. In other words, you're in the delicate process of recovering from a horrendous relationship with a total bastard (Aries, Scorpio and Pisces spring to mind here, for no apparent reason).

Who better than Taurus to charge into your life and help put you on the straight and narrow? The one man in the universe who seriously knows what's good for you and goes about giving it to you, no matter how many times you tell him to sod off . . . (At this point we could cut an interminably long rant short by saying Hitler was a Taurus. But we can't as the small army of the bloody Taurean bastards breathing down our necks won't let us) . . . Therefore, whilst you look on helplessly, Taurus will storm up and down the war office that's masquerading as a living-room, issuing arrest warrants, editorial comments and rent tribunal complaints on your behalf.

If you so much as *attempt* to get up to pour yourself another glass of his fortifying home brew, he'll bark at you to sit back down again as you don't need to stand on your own two feet whilst he's around. This usually has the effect of making you feel a bit redundant and fools him into dangerously misguided beliefs – like he's being incredibly useful. Don't think you're being unreasonable if, after a while, you feel like you don't have a thought of your own. Even if you did, Taurus wouldn't agree.

For argument's sake, let's say that whilst gulping down the twelfth dodgy beer he's brought, you chance upon the Virgin Mary glowering virtuously above the drinks cabinet. After you excitedly tell him about your immaculate discovery, he'll declare there's no such thing as God and you must be on drugs (which is not far from the truth since you've doubled your lithium intake in the vague hope you'll accidentally overdose).

However, you still have some of your faculties intact, one of which is pride. But even when you cross yourself, stand tall and point to Our Mary, Mother of God, whilst waving your diploma in Astrophysics, your degree in Visual Arts and your Masters in Biblical

Communications under his nose, he'll still insist you don't know what you're talking about. As far as Taurus is concerned, you're completely incapable of saying or doing anything by yourself. That's where he comes in. Again.

You casually mention that now you've got your PhD in Social Sciences and once you can face people again, you think it might be quite nice to have a career. Before you know it, there's a party plan rep making nuisance calls and a DSS officer dropping by to advise you on how to make buckets of dough being a domestic helper. (Taurus is a tad old-fashioned that way. Career girls aren't his cup of tea unless they actually make it for a living.)

You mention in passing that once you've got over your fear of wide open spaces, you'd quite like a holiday some time in the near future. Done. Booked. Paid for. Where? Why do you need to know? What's wrong with Poland? You'll like it. They don't eat much either.

You then let slip that, one day, when you're well enough, you might like to have a baby. Lo and behold, he waltzes into the bedroom waggling a thermometer, plotting your biorhythms and methodically filling in the appropriate forms to ensure Taurus Junior isn't left off the waiting list for Scouts.

The Taurus bastard is so big on practicalities that before too long he'll be making your toes curl, which the doctors say is an encouraging sign since they had resigned themselves to you being a complete vegetable for the rest of your life.

You wouldn't mind so much if he came up with solutions in a less predictably earnest and efficient manner. Then at least there'd be a bit of gratuitous excitement, a spot of feckless recklessness to enjoy from the comfort of your coma. But to put it as politely as possible, Taurus is one of life's plodders. And whilst slow and steady may win the master race, it's pretty goddamn torturous to watch or to participate in (which is probably why you're still on the lithium and have quietly developed a methadone habit as well).

Paradoxically, when he's not running – and therefore ruining – your life for you, the Taurus bastard is busy being chronically lazy. When it comes to doing things for himself he won't move unless he has to (i.e. to the fridge, the fridge or the fridge). If he lives by himself, don't be ecstatic when he invites you over to his place. It'll look like a bomb's hit it – and this may very well be the case if he still lives in that bunker in Berlin.

His sloth-like ways do not bode well for what we will generously describe as your 'sex life' with him. Though Taurus likes to be in control when upright, he'll always allow you to be on top in bed. Indeed, he's so bone idle the only kind of rapid movement you're ever likely to experience is when your eyes are blinking in your sleep.

Propaganda issued from the Earth Sign camp decrees that, yes, he can be a bit of a couch potato but he is incredibly loyal, so yah boo sucks. Since when loyalty has been such a hallowed virtue is completely beyond our realms of comprehension. That rare breed of man who is faithful usually expects it to be returned in spades. If you, understandably, like the odd bit of extracurricular nookie just for variety, forget it. Another guy so much as looks at you and he'll be dead where he stands.

As for you, well, Taurus won't tick you off immediately. He'll just keep your innumerable betrayals on his mental scoreboard. Then, when your quota's up, he'll dismiss you. Ruthlessly. This can get a bit confusing because the last straw could be the fact you didn't pick up the groceries on your way home (you've finally been allowed out on your own, as long as it's only to the corner shop). So you'll go through life believing Taurus dumped you because you forgot the milk, not because you were having it off with his best friend.

And whilst you can plead your case until the cows come home, once he's made up his mind about something, *nothing* will force him to reconsider. Threats involving kitchen appliances or power tools don't work unless a prison sentence for manslaughter seems preferable to putting up with his pigheadedness.

Be warned, though. If you *do* attempt to kill him and you *aren't* completely successful, he'll hold it against you for the rest of your life. When Taurus has a gripe about something, you will never, *ever* hear the end of it. On and on and on he'll go – he got rejected from art college, his mother didn't love him, his Alsatian got run over (repeat as often as you like for maximum desired effect).

Our only advice here is to make the most of your rapidly deteriorating mental health by raving like a maniac. That means he'll be forced to stop doing likewise and be helpful for once by rushing round trying to find you a good psychiatrist.

How to spot one

The odd-shaped skull, slightly bovine features and pot-belly are usually dead give-aways. However, if he's also got a moustache and salutes you with his arm raised straight in front of him, call Mossad immediately.

Where to find one

Standing over you, lying under you or sitting in a seat on behalf of a completely daft political party. If by fat chance he's running anywhere it'll be on doctor's orders only.

How to intrigue one

Look as unfetching as you can in your wheelchair. When he smiles at you, turn a blind eye and stare pointedly at the golden Labrador seated next to you. When he doesn't get the hint and instead says, '*Guten morgen*', pretend to be deaf and use sign language to make him go away. When he still refuses to take 'fuck off, Adolf' for an answer and persists in asking you out, pretend you're also mute so you don't have to say 'yes'.

The first date

He'll push you kicking and screaming in your wheelchair to a beer festival. There he'll devour all the bratwurst and sauerkraut within gobbling range whilst you drink the lager tent dry in a dismal attempt to forget.

When to do the deed

Join the resistance and don't.

When to pop the question

When you're fed up with all the vicarious thrills and tumultuous times provided by less dependable but ultimately more desirable bastards. And only after you've quit your drug problem and practised your goose-step so you can walk down the aisle in a straight line.

If he dumps you

He won't. Tenacity is his *only* virtue. Dump *him* instead.

If you dump him

He'll patiently wait for you to realise your disastrous mistake. When you don't, he'll patiently wait until you do.

The Virgo Bastard
AUGUST 24–SEPTEMBER 23

EVER WONDERED WHAT GOES ON IN THE MIND OF a serial killer? Find out what Interpol has been trying to discover for years and date a Virgo bastard. Because, if you're going to be a successful psychopath, you have to:

❑ enjoy repeating the same tedious task in the same mind-numbing fashion;

❑ have an unhealthy obsession with the little details – details normal people can't be bothered with because they've got lives;

❑ be too thick-skinned to notice people crossing to the opposite side of the street when they see you;

❑ write checklists to ensure you do everything you keep threatening to do.

If you're currently in love with Virgo and you don't want to believe the truth ('he seems such a nice, quiet, unassuming kind of guy'), pick up any detective novel that features an ice-pick-wielding nutter and then try telling us he doesn't remind you of someone you know and it's all just a bunch of alarming coincidences.

Let's face it, massive generalisations and sweeping statements aside, the circumstantial evidence is overwhelming. Like the odd little habits Serial Killer/Virgo picked up in childhood. Even if you replace pulling wings off insects with stamp collecting, exchange bed-wetting for train-spotting and substitute a fascination with lighting fires for an unhealthy interest in algebra, you've got to admit the similarities are pretty disturbing.

This budding Bates is so spine-tinglingly awful, his own mother encourages him to take sweets off strangers and tries to lose him in shopping centres. If she's lucky – and he takes her advice about only crossing roads when the red man is flashing – she won't have to put up with him telling her how to defrost her fridge-freezer correctly.

Then there's the usual (*yawn*) teenage angst that turns the slightly creepy, pale, skinny youth into a veritable walking time-bomb. A traumatic experience like the fact people make it patently obvious they hate his guts because he's so bloody anal is usually a good place to start. His well-scrubbed, clean-cut features and neatly creased trousers make it only right that other boys should want to beat him up. The fact that he can't understand why they pick on him gives them all the more reason to do so.

And who can blame the girls for refusing to kiss him behind the school lavatory? To do so means he'd be close enough to scrutinise them. Serial Killer/Virgo is such a nitpicker he won't just see the spots on their chins, he'll also see the blackheads, whiteheads, open pores and broken capillaries. And if he does happen to be staring deeply into their eyes, it's a dead cert he's moonlighting as an iridologist.

No wonder the adult version is so unsuccessful with women (which, by the way, is another tired excuse the average psycho uses to justify his anti-social behaviour when the overweight, chain-smoking, alcoholic/detective eventually catches up with him). That penetrating Virgo gaze will turn you into a quivering mass of neuroses in no time. Yes, you could choose to do it with the lights off, but then you wouldn't be able to see him reach under the bed for his icepick.

It goes without saying he'll also put your domestic habits under the microscope. If you're the kind of girl who thinks housework means waving a vacuum cleaner in the general vicinity of the living-room, you're going to drive Virgo insane (which takes quite a lot of doing since 'drive' and 'Virgo' don't exactly go hand in hand). Likewise, if your idea of cleaning the bathtub consists of chucking in a bar of soap whilst douching, prepare for problems.

Of course, we're not for one moment suggesting you'll end up on his things-to-do list. And look on the bright side anyway: ending up dead will be a lot less painful in the long run than putting up with his incessant nagging. Virgo's obsession with *your* domestic hygiene borders on the pathological. The reason for this is obvious to everyone save fat detectives stalking serial killers.

Leave him to his own devices and he's wont to sit quite happily in his own mess for months at a time. However, if *you* keep his house sparkling clean, the people from forensic aren't going to be able to pick up the stray hair, blood and bone off the living-room carpet.

Having said all this, there is one vice authors habitually omit when describing Virgo's less endearing qualities. And that's because even they are too appalled to bring themselves to put it down on paper. Whippings and beatings they can happily handle. Lashing of livers and buckets of blood they can just about stomach. But let's not talk about [*insert stage whisper here*] his spending habits.

It would be a gross miscarriage of justice to call

Virgo mean with money. 'Mean' is an inoffensive little word that cannot hope to conjure up the parsimonious ways of this bastard. Instead, try calling him 'an outrageous tightwad who would steal the coins out of a blind man's hat if he thought the poor beggar wasn't looking'.

Virgo is so careful with his cash, he never actually leaves home *with* it. However, he's quite willing to let you spend yours – usually on expensive suits for him to replace the bloodstained ones he's had to drop off at the drycleaners.

As with all his other bad behaviour, there is a deep-rooted psychological excuse for his skinflint shenanigans: since his clients don't pay him for the work he does on their behalf, nor do they leave him anything in their wills, he's bound to be financially bereft.

Indeed, to cut a long murder story short, the only things Virgo willingly spends his and/or your money on are personal grooming kits for him, household cleaning products for you and, yes, those infernal ice picks.

How to spot one

If he looks vaguely familiar, that's because he is. You probably saw an artist's sketchy impression on *Crimewatch* the night before and faintly remember words like 'bludgeoned', 'manhunt' and 'Virgo'.

However, he's much more attractive in the flesh. He's well groomed and often fair of hair – like most serial killers in most killer serials. Just look for the cool, calm, collected one doing nothing but staring disconcertingly at you from across the room.

Where to find one

Holding up bank queues querying bank charges. Loitering outside self-motivation seminars. Loitering inside the Territorial Army. In a public lavatory wiping the evidence off his hands. In a maximum-security psychiatric ward complaining the wardens put his jacket on back to front and, furthermore, it doesn't go with his trousers.

How to intrigue one

Mention your inheritance in casual conversation. At the same time run your finger seductively up and down the bar counter and comment upon the disgraceful amount of dust there.

The first date

When he eventually gets around to asking you out, he'll take you to one of those Hare Krishna centres where for less than fifty pence you can have all the lentils you do not wish to eat. (*Handy hint: don't insincerely offer to split the bill unless you genuinely want to get rid of all the small change in the bottom of your handbag.*) Be on your guard if, towards the end of the evening, he says he knows this great little spot for an after-dinner drink and it happens to be down a cellar, atop a cliff or up a dark alley.

When to do the deed

Don't. The Virgo bastard does for sex what mad cow disease did for beef on the bone.

When to pop the question

What question are we talking about here? 'When you polish your faucet in future can you also remember to clean the bathtub?', 'How come I'm paying for dinner again?' or 'Why do you wax the hair on your chest when you've got so little on your head?'

If he dumps you

Like most things in Virgo's life, he'll probably never get around to it. If he does, it's obviously because you didn't keep his shower recess clean enough or file his grocery receipts properly. Either that or you flicked through the mug-shots at the local police station, pointed to his face and said: 'That's him. That's the low-life who *loaned* me forty pence to make an emergency phone call after he attempted to hack me to death with an ice pick.'

If you dump him

He'll be ominously, quietly hurt. And just when you think you're rid of him, he'll appear from behind, accompanied by dodgy camera angles and predictable cello solo. Don't think he's hiding a bunch of flowers behind his back – flowers cost money. No, the thing in his hand behind his back is that goddamned ice pick again.

The Capricorn Bastard
DECEMBER 22–JANUARY 20

FINALLY, A MAN WHO TAKES RELATIONSHIPS seriously. Blessed with the heart of a loan shark, the humour of an undertaker and the sensitivity of a tax auditor, Capricorn takes *everything* seriously.

His intentions towards you are entirely honourable. He is hard working and ambitious. He wants to get married and raise a family. He has no problem with the concept and implementation of commitment. He'll even be faithful to you – although this can't be guaranteed as he *is* a man.

And upon getting to know him better you'll find he also possesses all the charm and conversation of a cash register. (Well, you can't expect him to have all those virtues *and* a personality.) But before you jump up and down in orgiastic delight at the thought of spending time with him, there is a catch. There's something he has to do prior to whisking you off into the sunset to issue joint financial statements together: he has to check your credit rating. And no, he's not joking. He never jokes about money. Or anything else, come to think of it.

If you happened to be born with silver cutlery anywhere near your mouth and you have an obscenely large trust fund to your name, you're laughing (and he may even smile) all the way to the bank and the joint savings account. However, don't assume he's only interested in you for your inheritance. Such an assumption would be a gross misjudgement of character. The truth is, if you'd won your money in a lottery or made it yourself through hard work or shrewd investments, he'd still be interested in it.

And it'd be unfair to say money is the only thing that matters to Capricorn. He is mostly human and understands your money alone will not ensure his happiness. That's why your social standing is just as important to him. He'll not only be interested in you for what you have but for who you are, who you know, who your parents are, what they have, who they know and what you can all do for him. (And you thought men were only interested in *one* thing.) Anyway, he's not searching for the love of his life. He first found that as a small child, beneath the cushions of his parents' couch. And he will always be true to it. Besides, marriage isn't about love; it's about making money.

Capricorn is the reason finishing schools still exist. You know, those wonderfully traditional educational institutions that concern themselves with taking affluent, intelligent young women and making them completely useless for anything other than marriage. As well as offering the only recognised diploma course in *Understanding Cutlery*, these outrageously expensive and usually Swiss schools take all the hard work out of finding a partner for Capricorn.

The cost involved ensures only the very wealthy and socially well placed can afford to send their daughters there. This eliminates all unsuitable candidates. Then the suitable are vigorously trained to eliminate any beliefs they may have in gender equality or themselves.

First you learn to cook the kind of meals which take days or sometimes weeks of preparation – the results of which can be ruined in a few seconds by an aeroplane passing overhead. This is to keep you occupied after you are married and is also impressive when you have to throw dinner parties for your Capricorn-bastard-husband's business contacts.

Then you'll learn to cultivate/fake an appreciation of the arts and an understanding of politics and world affairs so you can make seemingly intelligent conversation whilst you are cooking for and serving the guests. At these dinner parties you could translate a business deal for your huband with one of the five major European languages you picked up between classes at finishing school. And as for the etiquette required to know exactly where at the table to seat an earl or a prime minister if a member of the royal family is also coming – well, that was covered in your first year when you studied *Introduction To Seating Royalty, Nobility and Important Public Officials*.

Along with *How To Lose A Tennis Match To A Man Without Him Suspecting You Are Throwing The Game To Save His Ego*, *The Art of Table Setting II (Advanced Course)*, *How To Be Patronised Gracefully* and countless other vital business courses, you will be taught to walk, to speak and to dress yourself properly. Sure, you may have learnt to do these things when you were eighteen months old but these schools don't take any chances. You will also be taught needlework – majoring in embroidery. We have no idea why.

But the most important thing you can do at these schools is to mix and become lifelong friends with all those other obscenely rich, pedigreed girls. You don't actually have to like them, you just have to kiss the air around their cheeks for the rest of your life. They, like you, will all go on to marry Capricorn bastards to whom you can introduce your Capricorn bastard.

These bastards will then form a boys' club where they can compare their incomes, golf swings and penises (they'll call it networking) to their hearts' content. Naturally, you won't be allowed to join as you don't have a penis and, as you're married to a Capricorn bastard, you'll only ever get one at the end of each financial year – if it was a successful one.

You are now a graduate of the you-can-never-be-too-thin-too-rich-too-blonde-or-too-tanned school of thought and you are accomplished enough to take up that all-important position of catering to Capricorn's whims. You're a perfect wife: you have absolutely no marketable skills so you'll have nothing better to do than to further your husband's career. In other words, you will be *bored*. In your perfect house with your perfect husband and your perfect children. Bored with your air-and-arse-kissing friends who are all as boring as you. Bored with all the affairs you've had with the hired help because your husband only has sex if the Windsor-Kennedy-Smythe-Joneses are doing it too (and they never get around to it either). Bored, blonde, rich and eminently socially acceptable. May we suggest slipping into a coma to get through it all. No one will ever notice the difference.

NB: In more astrologically qualified circles there are a couple of widely repeated rumours about Capricorn. Firstly, deep down, he is reported to have the romantic soul of a poet – we find this one very hard to believe. And secondly, once he achieves his financial and social ambitions and retires, he becomes a lot of fun to have around. We can neither deny nor confirm these astrological rumours as we think life is too short to spend it with a Capricorn bastard.

How to spot one

Sneak a look under his bed to find his favourite well-thumbed and stained copies of the *Financial Times*.

Where to find one

At graduation ceremonies at finishing schools. In buildings where large sums of money are stored. Scanning the social pages for recently separated women with impressive names and even more impressive divorce settlements.

How to intrigue one

Accidentally drop your investment portfolio (the one embossed with your heavily hyphenated name) and make sure it is substantial enough to register on the Richter scale when it hits the ground. As he is helping you retrieve it, spill some large denomination notes into his lap whilst also dropping the names of all the big important people that Daddy-the-media-magnate-or-hotel-tycoon-or-reigning-monarch-of-a-small-but-wealthy-and-tax-free-nation wants to introduce your future husband to.

The first date

He will use this first meeting to assess your suitability; to figure out whether or not you are a worthy investment; to see if you know the difference between a fish fork and a dessert fork. In fact, it'll be a lot like a job interview. (*Tip: Make sure you look like a million dollars. At least.*)

When to do the deed

Go snooping in his Filofax. He'll have it scheduled in. Or better yet, ask his personal assistant when he plans to seal the deal – she'll have a clearer idea of when he can fit himself in. (*Important note: On paper the Capricorn bastard is quite good at sex. He passed* Sleeping Your Way To The Top I & II & III *with flying colours at business school. However, everything was only taught in theory so don't be surprised if he has to use a Global Positioning System to find your erogenous zones.*)

When to pop the question

When you own at least 51 per cent of his corporation. He's not going to refuse his major shareholder. And even if he does, you have the deciding vote – so you can overrule him.

If he dumps you

This is a very good sign. It means he's getting serious about you. He's starting to negotiate. Have Daddy up the dowry and go back with a counter-offer.

If you dump him

He's financially secure enough to handle it. It's all there in the prenuptial agreement; the dowry was non-refundable in the event of disagreement. As for the rest of your inheritance – well, he'll just have to marry another retirement plan.

We-Love-You-We-Love-You-Not

AIR SIGNS

Gemini ★ Libra ★ Aquarius

Possessing a remarkable inability to stick to anything for long, Air Sign bastards make incredibly poor long-term partners and even poorer wall decorations. They have little or no idea how to conduct themselves in a relationship and only have a vague inkling of what a relationship actually is. Yet this doesn't prevent them from trying to pass themselves off on the unsuspecting, astrologically unaware as suitable lovers and partners.

Air Sign bastards are game to try anything once. For a short time. But ask them to commit to anything longer than a lunch and they'll literally disappear into thin air. They were born with an innate fear of commitment and, more importantly, an ability to sense its looming presence far enough away to always stay one step ahead of its clutches.

So, it stands to reason: if you require attentiveness, sympathy or even just the physical presence of partners, don't go running to Air Sign bastards. Firstly, you won't be able to catch them. Secondly, they're not really interested in getting to know you any better. Though, it's not that they don't care enough. It's just that they don't care at all.

But the really sad thing is, Air Sign bastards lack the vital organ – a heart – necessary for you to inflict emotional trauma upon them and they are never around long enough for you to attempt lasting physical harm.

The Gemini Bastard
MAY 22–JUNE 21

RELATIONSHIPS JUST DON'T HOLD MUCH APPEAL for a Gemini bastard. The hours are terribly inconvenient. Intimacy is stifling. Monogamy sucks. Rules are stupid. And as for the thought of spending time alone with you – that's absolutely terrifying. See, you could get too close. Then you'd want to know what's deep down inside of him. And he's afraid to show you because he's not quite sure what's down there himself. (Our bets are on a primordial black hole.) This is why he'll prefer to keep you as just an acquaintance. Even after you're married to him.

But there's good reason for his behaviour: *he's possessed.* No, don't call the exorcist. This isn't a medieval chant, holy water and crucifix thing. It's worse. A Gemini bastard has many demons – a multitude of personalities living inside him, each of whom qualifies as a bastard in his own right.

Firstly, there's Mikey. He gets to go first because he has the earliest bedtime. He's eternally four years old and alternates between being a total cherub and the brat from hell – the former when he's asleep and the latter when he's awake. He makes all the major financial, family and relationship decisions. In fact, he handles everything of importance. When the rare occasion arises on which he needs advice he turns to Zoltan (see page 69). Otherwise he is a normal four-year-old – incapable of taking care of himself. Spending time with him is like any normal four-year-old play session; it ends in tears. Your tears. Of sheer frustration.

A psychiatrist would probably diagnose Mikey as a symptom of the fact that Gemini doesn't want to grow up and take responsibility for his life. Whether or not this is true, Mikey is a minor and as such cannot be held responsible for his actions either by you or the law.

Next up is Tony, a real piece of work. He's a used car salesman. A very, very good one. He's the reason you're in a relationship with a Gemini bastard in the first place. He's very good at selling things nobody wants. When you confront Gemini and tell him you don't believe he (*sob*) truly cares about you, Tony jumps in with something along the lines of: 'But Sarah, the idea of life without you is inconceivable to me. You are my reason for living, the most important person in my world,' etc. He'll seem so sincere and convincing you'll believe him, even though your name is Rachel.

Oh, and have you met Frank? You'll just *love* Frank. He works the room for a living. He's the life and soul of a double-vodka-martini cocktail party. He's intensely interested in people other than you. For up to five minutes at a time. If he seems superficial, that's only because he is. The 'other people' adore Frank and invite him everywhere, encouraging him to be even more annoying.

Walter, on the other hand, is dreadfully unpopular. He's nervous, jumpy and always in need of a good stiff drink. He appears whenever there's a tense or stressful situation and runs around making an awful commotion without actually being of any use.

Charles is infinitely more useful. A brilliant prosecuting attorney always is. Whenever Gemini finds he has painted himself into a corner (and you think you've finally pinned him down) Charles comes to the rescue. He is logical, cynical and heartless. He can make you admit to committing crimes you've never even heard of. Unfortunately for justice, he uses his formidable talent to prosecute the victim. And in the case of dating Gemini, you are *always* the victim.

Last and least is Zoltan. Master Sorcerer, Dragon Slayer, Defender of the Universe and Keeper of the

Legendary Golden Orb (the one with the sticker that says 'For use in the event of the complete destruction of mankind. Press blue button to save world. If you feel like it'). We aren't really sure where Zoltan fits in. He is officially in charge of changing light bulbs, refilling ice cube trays and other light domestic chores (but, naturally, a man on whom the fate of the entire universe depends can't be expected to be good at mundane details). We also suspect he's the one responsible for listening when wives and girlfriends want to 'talk'.

So now you know, it's not that your Gemini bastard doesn't care about you, it's just that Zoltan is limited in what he can do to resolve your problems when he exists in another reality. Once you get those earthly problems out into deep space, they look kind of small and insignificant. And just how practical can you expect someone named Zoltan to be? (*Warning: Zoltan has been known to make the leap across the space–time continuum to go out on dates.*)

Mikey, Tony, Frank, Walter, Charles and Zoltan all interact with one another. They egg each other on, whip each other into mad frenzies and appear in random order to torment you. The medical term for this is Multiple Personality Disorder.

Because Gemini lives amid this turmoil he will continually change his ideas and opinions. What he says today won't mean anything tomorrow and it probably didn't mean much today either. You could see this as a natural result of him having to deal with his conflicting personalities. Or you could see it as a result of him being a two-faced, two-timing, lying bastard. But, thankfully, there are a few things guaranteed to remain constant in your Gemini bastard. These things are the traits all his personalities have in common: they are never ever wrong. They are never ever at fault. And they will never ever have an attention span of longer than fifteen seconds.

So if Gemini plans to go to the movies with you a week ahead of time and actually follows through, see it as a long-term commitment (sorry, this is as good as it gets) and send out the wedding invitations.

Once you are married and you decide you and the kids would really like to see your Gemini bastard more than once a week – though most likely this will be enough – all is not lost. Just get work experience as a warden in a maximum-security facility where the inmates are constantly trying to escape. Then you'll know how to deal with him. Or pack up the family and move to Alcatraz. They'll put you all in separate cells but it will be the only way you'll ever know where your Gemini bastard is at all times.

How to spot one

Gemini is particularly hard to spot. He'll be standing in front of you, talking at you in one instant and he'll be a blur in the distance the next. This is a real problem if you want to shoot him.

Where to find one

On television chat shows, on psychiatrists' couches, on the phone to recorded-message services or at a McDonald's drive-through having an interesting discussion with the intercom. Basically, anywhere he can have a conversation without making an emotional commitment.

How to intrigue one

Don't require sympathy. Or consistency. Or fidelity. Or company. Don't ask where he is going. Or when he might be coming back. Or if he's coming back. And don't ever ask anything more emotionally demanding than 'How are you?' or 'Where did you get your shoes?'.

The first date

Enjoy it. He will actually pay attention to you as he isn't bored with you yet. (*Tip: To prolong his interest, try not to wear clothing more interesting than you are.*)

When to do the deed

As soon as possible. How often do you get the chance to indulge in group sex? (All Gemini's personalities take part in sex. This means he doesn't have to have an emotional obligation to you as you're technically sleeping with other people.)

When to pop the question

At times you'll see that, not-so-deep down, Gemini is truly committed to you. Like when he manages – without the help of cue cards – to remember the names of your three children. This is as good a time as any to bring up marriage. And unless you want your kids to resent you for not managing to marry their father within their lifetime, don't be too demanding. Holding out until he manages to put the right name to the right child is asking far too much.

If he dumps you

It doesn't mean he doesn't like you any more. He's just forgotten you, that's all. If you really miss him, engineer a chance meeting. You'll pique his interest as he'll find you vaguely familiar, reminding him of someone . . . hmmm . . . whom he can't quite place. Then you can start dating him all over again.

If you dump him

Gemini will suddenly discover he definitely does have deep feelings for you. Feelings you have hurt. Terribly. Irrevocably. His heart is shattered. His soul destroyed. His life meaningless. How could you do this to him, you . . . you . . . what was your name again?

The Libra Bastard
SEPTEMBER 24–OCTOBER 23

THE POOR, CONFUSED BASTARD. IT'S NOT *HIS* fault. Life in the modern world is getting more and more complex and there are so many *decisions* to make. He now has to decide between a half-flush and a full-flush every time he goes to the toilet. The stress is *unbelievable*.

So you can just imagine the pressure he's under when he has to decide whether or not to ask you out. What if he does, discovers he really likes you and wants to see you again? What if he sees you again and likes you even more? Then he'd have to keep on seeing you. Which would probably lead to a major commitment like marriage and kids. And he's not quite sure where to take the family on their annual holiday or where the boys should go to school.

What if you aren't the love of his life, but he marries you anyway? Then what would he do when the real love of his life comes along? What if he doesn't ask you out, and you turn out to be the woman of his dreams? Then he would spend his whole life knowing he let you go. So maybe he should ask you out just in case. But, then again, maybe it's better not to see the woman of his dreams on a daily basis because that would make it all so mundane and not a bit romantic.

And there's another thing to consider: *what if he asks you out and you say 'no'*?

It's a wonder Libra ever ends up in a relationship at all. But the truth is, he's always sort-of-involved or looking to be sort-of-involved. He wanders from relationship to relationship, pushing up the country's divorce rate. (Seven out of ten dead-end relationships involve a Libra bastard. The other three mainly concern Pisces bastards.)

All the while, Libra is hoping the right girl will come along and make a decision for him. And even if *she* never comes along, he's sort-of-sure there's someone better than you just around the corner. It's a real pity he doesn't just go and look around the corner. Because he might just get mugged, and then you wouldn't have to put up with him turning his overworked little mind on to everything that's wrong with you.

He'll find plenty to be concerned about. Of course,

he'll never voice any of these worries. Somehow you'll just *know* there's something wrong. You'll *know* that you don't measure up to the girl on the latest *Sports Illustrated* swimsuit edition cover. And you'll *know* that he's not happy about it. But on the upside, at least you'll never have to worry about Libra questioning your integrity, your morals or the beliefs you hold dear. Your goals and aspirations are similarly beyond him. Let's just say that if Libra was a swimming-pool there wouldn't be a deep end. His concerns about you only ever have to do with the way you look, sound, dress or act.

For instance: what if you don't age well? Will your blonde streaks still look good when you're thirty-five? Will you put on weight in the next fifty years? Will your voice get annoying? Should you wax more often? Does that pink polish on your toes really go with that dress? Is that dress tight enough? Is that dress too tight? Does that dress make your bum look big? Is your bum too big? And is that *cellulite* on your bum?

Then there's always the possibility that when he's out on a date with you, you will both bump into a lonely supermodel (who has too much integrity to muscle in on another woman's date). Or a visiting group of Miss Universe contestants or a bus full of unchaperoned sixteen-year-old schoolgirls – who would, of course, be all over him if only you weren't around.

With all these weighty matters to sort out it's no wonder Libra takes a very long time to make any kind of a move. Of course, you could take matters into your own hands (which is generally what women do with Libra bastards, unless they are very young and have plenty of time to waste). And he'll go along with it as it allows him to put off making a decision about you. But the fact Libra willingly comes on dates with you, moves in with you, or even marries you doesn't mean anything. He's just procrastinating.

But because it takes him so long to make up his mind about you (anywhere up to twelve years), you will actually think you are in a secure, committed and happy relationship. Unless you're a mind reader, you'll be taken in by the bland expression constantly on his face and never guess that he's still trying to decide whether or not to *date* you. After all, you have been living together for four years.

So when he actually decides he doesn't want to date you and leaves, it will come as a bit of a surprise. (But his timing will be impeccable. He'll do it when you can least understand it: just after you leave high school; just after you've introduced him to your parents; just after you've shown all your friends the big diamond ring he gave you; just after you find out you are pregnant; just after you move in together; just after your career takes off; just before (or directly after) you get married; or just after the kids have all left for college.) And you'll be completely flabbergasted.

Don't get mad at him, though. The Libra bastard doesn't respond well to screaming and sobbing and smashing crockery. If he thinks you're putting on what he considers to be an excessive display of emotion (or an excessive amount of weight) he'll disappear quietly out of your life and find someone, well, nicer. Someone who doesn't make his ears bleed or head ache, someone who won't question him or demand that he thinks about anything more complicated than which shade of lipstick she should wear. That she is also seventeen, with large breasts, long blonde hair, a lingerie modelling contract and happens to be a complete twit, well, these things are just bonuses.

But don't worry, you won't miss him once he's dumped you. He'll come back around, keeping tabs on you. (He still hasn't made up his mind about you *completely*.) He'll also continue to sleep with you if you let him and bitch about all the problems he's having with his new, extremely young, girlfriend, if you let him. These will mostly be problems about her occasionally immature behaviour and what he should wear to her school dance. (His behaviour in this situation should give you a pretty good idea of what he was doing when he caught up with his ex-girlfriends while he was dating you.)

Tip: *If you happen to be an elderly woman with billions of dollars, we have it on very good authority that Libra bastards make excellent toy boys or pets.*

How to spot one

He's the charmingly boyish, well-dressed one – with the nicely blow-dried hair and the vacant look on his face.

Where to find one

At forks in the road, in modern, dual-flushing toilets or on the judging panel of a Miss Universe contest. In fact, anywhere there are trivial decisions to be made.

How to intrigue one

Appear to be Gisele fresh from a fashion shoot. Appear to be carefree and unused to heavy thoughts. Appear to be very young with overdeveloped breasts. Then wait with the patience of an angel for him to make a move.

The first date

The first date with Libra is usually quite wonderful. He'll take you to a popular place where the wine (you chose it), wit (yours, that is) and conversation (yours again) will flow. He'll even pick up the bill with a generous flourish (he's seen other men do it). So why did you have to go and spoil it all by asking if he's going to call you again?

When to do the deed

Hold out for as long as possible – it's not like you'll be missing anything. Stretch it out for a year or two whilst he's busy deciding whether or not to date you. In any case, it'll end up being your decision and therefore your fault.

When to pop the question

When you want the relationship to end.

If he dumps you

This means he has met somebody else, as he's incapable of ending a relationship without help from a grown-up. If you try and get him back, it'll just confuse him. Whether or not he goes or stays, he'll claim you forced him into the decision. Best to leave well enough alone.

If you dump him

Libra will be settled, happily or not, with a new partner before the ink is dry on the Dear (insert-appropriate-Standard-Boy's-Name-here) letter you send him. You could feel outraged at the speed with which he forgets you. Then again, you'll find it impossible to continue to take him that seriously.

The Aquarius Bastard
JANUARY 21–FEBRUARY 19

AQUARIUS IS THE MOST REASONABLE BASTARD you'll ever encounter. He'll even agree he is a bastard. If he was born out of wedlock then he is one by definition and if you want to call him a bastard for other, more personal, reasons he'll certainly allow you your opinion.

And he won't, like other bastards and real astrologers, dismiss this book as amateur astrological crap. In his mind every viewpoint gets a hearing, every belief system has some legitimacy. To top things off, he's likely to be annoyingly good-looking (well, there goes your ability to remain objective). Cuteness aside, open-mindedness and tolerance in a bastard has its own set of problems. A very different set of problems than you're used to. In fact, after years of dealing with men who don't listen to you when the football game, the television or the fridge is on, you'll be totally unequipped to deal with Aquarius.

Standard forms of male manipulation (e.g. screaming like a banshee or carefully planned sex deprivation) don't work on Aquarius. He is more profound and more complex than the average bastard. Whilst normal little boys were constructing little Lego spacecraft piloted by little Lego spacemen from the planet Biffo, Aquarius junior was delving into the mysteries of existence. True, he did it via television and comic books, but his sincere intention to discover the deeper meaning of life was there. The distressing thing is that he managed to find depth and reality in *The Brady Bunch* and in the Bat Cave and will regale you with their profundity.

Spending his formative years as a weirdo has resulted in the adult Aquarius male holding radical beliefs. Being a radical is quite easy. He doesn't have to stick to one system of thought as, say, the poor communists do. He can adopt an ideology to fit his mood and situation. And he'll be happy as long as it allows him to oppose some commonly held belief – your belief in marriage, for instance.

Taking the opposing stance is the foundation of all his beliefs. And once everybody else is a radical, left-wing, feminist-separatist-greenie-with-a-nose-ring, he'll become a conservative. The only thing he hates more than conservatism is to do what everybody else is doing. He prides himself on his otherness.

It follows, then, that his views on romantic relationships defy conventions and escape comprehension. See, commitment limits personal growth for both partners. Marriage is an outmoded aspect of organised religion and is no more than a pricey piece of paper in today's world, and love (like currency) should be circulated for the benefit of everybody – not hoarded in a miserly way to be doled out regularly to one individual.

Of course, that one individual – you, in this case – may have different thoughts on the matter. In theory, his beliefs are fine. There is nothing wrong with seeing each human being as a free and responsible agent determining their own path through life. It's just not terribly warm and fuzzy. And it presents some practical difficulties. Like, where do you, the people-carrier and the 2.3 children fit in?

That's a huge problem with most philosophers – they don't include a section entitled 'How to Nab a Man and Keep Him' in their manifestos. (They haven't included other basic human needs either – like clothes shopping and trashy television shows.)

Understandably, you'll come to the conclusion Aquarius is operating on a completely different, totally baffling level. But the thing is, he does believe in love. The all-encompassing kind. The noble feeling of compassion for one's fellow men – which unites people for the greater good of humanity. The selfless, undemanding emotion . . . (sorry, we have to stop here – we're feeling slightly nauseous). And of course he loves you. Aren't you a fellow inhabitant of earth? How could he *not* love you?

What Aquarius fails to understand is that loving all human beings equally only ever worked for Jesus Christ, and Jesus Christ was the Son of God. How secure are you going to feel dating a mere mortal who practises this? And as Aquarius is busy spreading his love among humanity, you can't even cause a scene about it. Making a fuss would mean you were jealous. And jealousy is a primitive, self-destructive emotion. You must have an incredibly low opinion of yourself to even entertain such a feeling – you really do have some major self-doubts, don't you? Perhaps you should discuss this problem of yours with Aquarius because he really does want to help.

That's the problem. Aquarius has noble, humane reasons for everything he does. Reasons which make you look selfish and uncaring for putting your needs before those whose needs are greater than your own. Shame on you. When was the last time *you* built a well for a Third World village? (Although now and then, amongst his great rhetoric, you'll get a sneaking feeling all of this is just an elaborate hoax designed to cover up his fear of commitment.)

You can't even nail your Aquarius bastard for sexism – he'll show you up. He's read all those books you bought to place on your shelves for decorative purposes. He'll dismiss your rantings as a product of the victim-feminism so prevalent these days and so damaging to the real feminist cause.

Face it – he's a better feminist than you are. He's spent years pondering the male paradox (i.e. how can one be male, loaded up with testosterone and still be a decent human being?). Hence his evasive, noncommittal behaviour towards you. He's actually trying to make up for all that his gender has done. The less time he spends with you, the less chance he has to undermine your gender by treating you like an unpaid domestic servant – as men are biologically inclined to do. And he won't be guilty of treating you as a sex object if he doesn't have sex with you regularly. Instead, he can spread his natural male instinct to objectify women over a number of them, thus diluting its damaging effect. See how concerned he is about you? Are you feeling grateful yet?

Well, if you aren't, don't get any bright ideas about trying to talk your Aquarius bastard around to your point of view unless you were captain of the debating team at secondary school. Just adopt a poverty-stricken child, hug a tree, rescue rabbits, protest against anything owned by Phillip Morris and go with the flow. Or if you want to be rid of your Aquarius bastard: purchase shrink-wrapped fruit, wear fur and say how great it would be to be as skinny as the children in the World Vision ads, except for all the flies and heat and stuff.

How to spot one

Find him attractive and he'll be completely oblivious to your existence. Ignore him and he'll be all over you. Yes, we know, we've just described the behaviour of almost any man – so also look for an unhealthy gleam in his eye (as seen in the eyes of members of religious cults or people who live in small, padded rooms with locks on the outside).

Where to find one

Look in the exalted circles of Nobel laureates, inventors-of-things-that-help-mankind and great humanitarians to find your very own Aquarius bastard. Or look in the nearest looney bin (there are even more of them to choose from there). And if all else fails, look in the little rubber boats that chase Japanese whaling ships or leaky oil tankers; there'll be at least one half-drowned Aquarius on board.

How to intrigue one

Talk about some really interesting things you've done; like the time you restored peace in the Middle East; how you invented a cure for cancer; or when you discovered and communicated with a new form of life in the next galaxy – stuff like that. (*Tip: In general conversation, try not to come across as too ideologically unsound.*)

The first date

It probably won't be a 'date' as such. He's much more interested in you as a person and will ask you out on that pretext. After a few friendly encounters he'll notice you are a girl – you can then move things along from there.

When to do the deed

There is no need to abide by convention for this or any other aspect of your dealings with Aquarius. But do it discreetly so he doesn't notice. He'd hate to think he was taking advantage of you. (*NB: To save you from disappointment, be aware that when Aquarius mentioned The Big Bang Theory he wasn't referring to his sexual performance.*)

When to pop the question

Never, under any circumstances, do this. It will alert him to the fact you think of the relationship as more than just friendship. However, if you happen to be a member of an oppressed minority group, you stand a good chance of getting an Aquarian bastard to the altar – he won't want to be guilty of discrimination.

If he dumps you

He'll never really dump you. He'll always value you as a person. He'll just stop having sex with you – so the relationship will hardly change.

If you dump him

He'll take it philosophically and figure it was for the best anyway. But he'll ask if you can still be friends and won't be able to understand why you slam the door/hang up the phone/shoot him in the kneecap.

Don't-Hate-Us-'Cos-We're-Wishy-Washy

WATER SIGNS

Cancer ★ Scorpio ★ Pisces

For 'deep, sensitive and sensual' read 'secretive, paranoid and seriously perverted'. Water Sign bastards are to be avoided at all costs. They're deceitful, highly strung deviants who are hard to pin down except to a mattress.

Yes, Water Sign bastards *can* be very deep, sensitive and sensual. Because they're so *deep* they can look within themselves and see what wretched failures they truly are. Because they're so *sensitive* they're acutely aware that women neither like nor respect them. And because they're so *sensual*, they'll make sure you feel their torment too.

This is fine if you're a seriously co-dependent type who likes feeling maladjusted all the time. Because, in a pathetic attempt to bolster their own self-esteem, Water Sign bastards end up sucking every last drop of self-respect out of you. Without you, they're nothing. Of course, with you they're nothing either. But that's beside the point.

Fortunately for you, Water Sign bastards have very strong suicidal tendencies. Equally as unfortunately for you is that whilst they are wont to sit on top of very high kerbs and threaten to jump off, they never have the guts nor good manners to follow through.

The Cancer Bastard
JUNE 22–JULY 23

Dear Mother

I hope you are well. I am doing fine but wish you were here. A weekend away seems such a long time. Have just met a girl who I think could be the one. Like you, she is really pretty and really nice. I am sure the two of you will get on like a house on fire. Your ever-devoted son,

Cancer

WELL, WE COULDN'T HAVE PUT IT BETTER OURSELVES. You're the house. She's the fire. And guess which one of you ends up the worst for wear?

To be fair, though, every mother openly loves her son and therefore secretly resents his girlfriend. In return, every son secretly loves his mother and openly resents his girlfriend. But any boy should have the decency to look visibly embarrassed when Mummy combs his hair and wipes his face with a hanky laced with her own spit. When he's *thirty-eight*.

However, we're not talking about a grown man here, are we? We're talking about Cancer. So if you've just fallen in love with one, best of luck. Hopefully the old bag is dead. Because if she is still rattling around, you don't stand a bloody chance. The Cancer bastard's relationship with mother is the keystone to his existence. His ties to the apron strings make Oedipus look like a well-balanced, independent type who left home at an early age and only occasionally remembered to send his mother a birthday card.

Either Cancer dotes on mother to death and no other women can come betwixt, or else he hates her guts and therefore detests that 51 per cent of the population capable of bearing children.

It's probably better he leans towards the latter because that way he'll be so repellent you won't want to go anywhere near him. Unfortunately, he's more likely to be trotting over to her coven on a regular basis, affording her the opportunity to watch every wrong move you make. And let us tell you now: *you won't be good enough for her son*. Which she will tell him. And then tell him to tell you. This is often why Cancer will put off introductions between the two of you for as long as possible, and it is the only aspect of his widespread gutlessness to be applauded and, indeed, encouraged.

To your face, Cancer's mother will be as sweet as pie. But when you've looked beyond the wart on the end of her nose and begun to watch very, very closely, you'll soon realise where the term 'son-of-a-bitch' comes from.

She'll generously load your plate with kilos of kilojoules in the hope you'll end up as fat as her. Then, after you politely refuse a second helping, she'll kindly inquire after your eating disorder.

When Cancer – who is in his highchair at the kitchen bench toying with his mashed steak away from the adults – looks certain to leap to your defence, she'll fix him with the kind of glare that makes you all of a sudden want to reach for the dictionary and find out what a 'gimlet' actually is.

She'll subliminally click her tongue when you let him get up to wash his own bowl and spoon. It goes without saying she'll be silently apoplectic when you pass him your plate to wash also. When she can bring herself to speak again, she will innocently ask you why women of today can never seem to hold on to their men. This will prompt you to wonder why you haven't yet seen hide nor hair of Cancer's father. (Popular myth says the Cancer bastard didn't have a father. Common legend has it he was spawned. Stark reality deems dad died years ago of filial disappointment.)

As things are now beginning to get a bit strained between you and his mum, Cancer will pull one of his infamous panic attacks. This translates into a very mild fever, the faintest hint of the tremors, a few tears for dramatic effect and an inability to finish whatever he's doing at the time.

You won't help matters much by callously standing by whilst mother rushes to his side, clears his air passage of any obstructions, does a quick Heimlich manoeuvre and whips the dishcloth out of his shaking hands to do the dishes for him.

How were you to know about the dark family secret? No one told you Cancer was struck down at a tragically young age with mad cow's disease, now more popularly known as mother-who-mollycoddles. To date, your idea of babying an adult male has been to chuck him a codeine capsule as you waltz out the door to that all-important meeting or party.

So, aggrieved you haven't given him the milk of human kindness he so richly deserves and Mother still provides by way of bottled formula, Cancer will proceed to do what he does best and have a 'mood'. The huffs, puffs and sulks of Cancer make his namesake seem like a really fun thing to have around. And just when you think the thing's in remission, he'll scowl for a change of scenery. Don't be tempted to ask what's wrong because he'll just say 'nothing'. Mother specifically told him not to talk to strangers. And, be reasonable, he's hardly had time to get to know you over the last three years, what with all that self-introspection he's had to do.

The only way to make amends is to buy him a really fabulous present on the way home – preferably something old and precious so he can be reminded of you-know-who. Naturally, if this can't be arranged, just slip him a cheque.

In order to keep him in the sheltered lifestyle she believes to be his birthright, Cancer's mother never charged him board. Therefore, Cancer has learnt over the years to enjoy hoarding money. And, since the brain-addled bat also discouraged him from being ambitious enough to get a well-paid career when he grew up (because then he might flee the nest), he's had to be extraordinarily mean in order to accumulate a lot of it.

On the off-chance he does lash out on you (a box of cheap chocolates is always an encouraging sign), he'll be so racked with worry about his profligate spending he'll secretly hold it against you for months. So if he does grudgingly proffer an extravagant gift, express your eternal gratitude, discreetly return it to the discount store from whence it came and surreptitiously deposit the money back into his bank account.

Of course, this is precisely what he wanted you to do but was too afraid to ask because then you might scold him for being a sneaky, selfish little brat and just wait until you tell Mummy Dearest. If there's one thing he's more terrified of than being upfront, it's the thought of *her* walking steadily towards him with grim expression and heavy wooden coathanger.

How to spot one

The grown man with the attributes of a vile child is invariably Cancer. If he's also wearing a nappy, back off. He's either too young for you – or too old.

Where to find one

In a bookstore asking for directions to the self-help section; in Oxfam shopping for your birthday present; out drinking with the lads just to prove he's one of them. (However, one alcoholic beverage too many [one] and he'll be whingeing about how hard it ish to find a woman who can live up to hish mothersh high expectashuns.)

How to intrigue one

Tell him you like his mother. Tell him you like him. Or be honest, straightforward and positive and tell both of them to drop dead.

The first date

He'll invite you over to dinner and cook for you because it's cheaper than going out. On the rare occasion he invites you to his mother's place, it'll only be because he still lives there.

When to do the deed

When he's declared his undying love. Which he will. Very quickly. He's a two-fingers-down-the-throat romantic who used to steal glances at his mother's Barbara Cartland novels when normal boys were shoplifting *Hustler*. Just don't be surprised when he takes his words back again the next morning – particularly after mother bangs on the bedroom door and asks if he's all right because she heard him moaning and groaning through the night and thought he might have an upset tummy.

When to pop the question

Never, ever, *ever* marry a Cancer bastard. Or else you'll be forced to become his surrogate mother because that's the only way you'll get his attention and her goat.

If he dumps you

He's doing you a big favour and since favours aren't his forte, you should be grateful. Of course, because the Cancer bastard doesn't like being alone with himself for too long (and who can blame him) he's bound to come crawling back.

If you dump him

He'll run bawling to Mummy and she'll make him demand back the presents he bought you with her pension – but you didn't want that *Cookery in 1,000 Easy Lessons* book anyway, did you?

The Scorpio Bastard
OCTOBER 24–NOVEMBER 22

ALL THOSE DARK, BROODING, MONOSYLLABIC types who fill the pages of cheap romance novels with their square jaws and piercing eyes are Scorpios. You know the story: boy meets girl. Boy tortures girl because of a series of very silly misunderstandings and because he enjoys it. Girl becomes a psychological wreck. Boy sweeps girl into his arms and mumbles something about undying love. (He has to sweep her into his arms because by this stage the poor woman has completely fallen apart.)

This is where the book ends. There is a very good reason for this. Mills & Boon know what is to come is far too awful to be published.

Yet this paperback ideal of love still manages to override the common sense of most women. We find the strong, silent, manipulative type irresistible. And we sit prettily on our hope chests with our long auburn curls in charming disarray, waiting breathlessly with much fluttering of eyelashes for Scorpio to stride into our lives. (*NB: Romantic heroes never walk, they always stride – manfully and purposefully. It's dreadfully tiring for them and it is one of the reasons why they are so moody and irritable.*)

And once a Scorpio bastard arrives? Well, there's nothing like a spot of good-old-fashioned bodice-ripping to get things started. Just swoon gracefully into his arms and let him have his way with you. Then have your head examined. The strong, silent type is what you should look for when purchasing white goods. These are desirable attributes in a washing machine, not in a man. And we guarantee you won't enjoy them in Scorpio.

He *is* strong. Much stronger than you. Which means when there's a fight, you'll lose. And he *is* silent. Which means communication within the relationship is going to be a little strained and one-sided. Holding back information is actually one of his favourite pastimes. Mostly because it upsets you.

What did you expect? Anyone described as 'dark' and 'brooding' is not going to be a naturally open, caring, sharing person. And Scorpio has a dark side that makes Darth Vader look like Mr Whippy. He'll hold a grudge against you until the day you die. (Your death will only appease him a little.)

However, you'll never even know he has a grudge against you. Say you flirt harmlessly with a work colleague of his at the office Christmas party. It won't cross your mind that Scorpio is upset about it until one fine day three years later when he retaliates by sleeping with your maid of honour and your sister just hours before he marries you. Scorpio will wait – decades, if necessary – for the chance to get his revenge when you're not paying attention.

Unfortunately, because of the amount of literature (if books featuring men in tight breeches on the cover count as literature) you've absorbed, you'll class all his behaviour as normal. You'll revel in all the angst. Being miserable all the time must mean it's true love. This is all so romantic. You'll even be flattered by his possessiveness (despite the fact you're not allowed to go anywhere or see anyone) as it means he can't bear to be without you. Of course, he can't bear to be with you either – not while you are still capable of independent thought and action. But don't worry, you won't be capable for much longer.

Scorpio will manipulate you until you become exactly what he wants you to be. Then he'll lose respect for you as you're so easily manipulated. Then he'll start looking around for someone else to manipulate. This is when you should start looking around too – for reputable psychiatric help. Because, in the midst of torturing you, Scorpio will suddenly turn into a model of gentleness and consideration. He'll even be kind to animals (standard behaviour for all romantic hero types – designed to suck you into believing they have a soft, sensitive side). Don't be fooled. It's just part of the callous game he's playing with your mental and emotional health. His objective is to annihilate you. But if he can make you believe he is incapable of such an act, it makes it so much more fun when he actually does destroy you.

And he will destroy you. It's what Scorpio does best. And besides, it's how he likes to spend his spare time. Once you are a broken mess on the floor he'll pick you up and glue you back together so you're whole once more and he can start all over again.

He takes his hobby very seriously. It brings him hours of enjoyment and allows him to explore his destructive talents. And you'll get something out of it too. A hobby of your own; a lifelong obsession with him – the worse he treats you the more you'll like him. Why, we don't know. Needless to say you'll be spending all your spare time in expensive 12-step programmes undergoing extensive counselling.

Check into group therapy when you find yourself getting upset just because he is sleeping with other women. It's really none of your business. You *are* only his girlfriend/wife/mother of his children. And anyway, you'll meet his mistress soon enough when she joins the group after she discovers he's doing the same thing to her. Then you can console each other about your mutual stupidity. You'll both be introduced to a nationwide Unhealthily Obsessed Co-dependent Support Network for women who have dated Scorpio. It comes complete with a 24-hour hotline, which you'll put to very good use. (This is a free-of-charge service, one of many sponsored by the Aspiring Romantic Novelists Association who use it for research purposes.)

The reason Scorpio inspires such obsessive behaviour is because he is so obsessive himself – about sex. He thinks about it twice as much as other men, which basically means it's on his mind all the time. Which makes him a complete pervert. Which for some strange reason makes women think he's sexy. Which therefore means he really can't help having sex with any woman who'll let him. (*Warning: Don't be tempted to have an affair yourself to get back at your Scorpio bastard. Right now, you're in no emotional state to witness a jealous streak the size of the San Andreas Fault. This is probably unnecessary advice as you won't have time between those ever-increasing therapy sessions and the compulsive shopping habit you recently developed. And let's face it, the nervous twitch and chronic alcoholism aren't exactly going to be attracting men in droves.)*

You can't win. You will never ever win. Scorpio won't let you. And you can't leave as he won't let you do that either. All you can do is keep going to therapy and continue to blame yourself. After all, you're the crazy, co-dependent one with a thing for sadistic bastards.

(Advice: If, even after reading this chapter, you still want to experience what it feels like to have a relationship with a Scorpio bastard, find a busy motorway and throw yourself under a large lorry. It will feel just like dating a Scorpio bastard but will be comparatively much less painful.)

How to spot one

When a Scorpio bastard looks at you, you will feel a strong urge to shed your underwear. He will have this baffling effect upon you even if you're in a very public place and you find him most unattractive.

Where to find one

Follow the trail of emotional wrecks to his door. Or better still, let him find you. Because then at least you won't be the one who started the relationship which ruined your life.

How to intrigue one

Be sunny and happy and full of life. He won't be able to resist the challenge of luring you to the pits of hell. Once there, just be whatever he wants you to be. Holding on to your personality will only cause you a lot of unnecessary pain.

The first date

Scorpio will charm you into submission. Or else he'll worm his way into your life and affections without you noticing – like cancer or some other terminal disease. And after just one date, he'll know everything there is to know about you and you'll know absolutely nothing about him. This sets the tone for the entire relationship.

When to do the deed

Because Scorpio has so many hidden agendas, you'll never be able to pick the right time. So go to bed when he wants to, generally just after you've been introduced. (*Tip: When you do it, make like a porn star but somehow give the impression you've never done it before.*)

When to pop the question

If you feel the inclination to do this, have yourself committed.

If he dumps you

Trying to exact revenge will only serve to amuse Scorpio as your attempts will seem so amateurish. Besides, he'll be flattered he still has total control over your emotions and your life. On the other hand, running after him doing your best impersonation of a doormat will only invite him to clean his boots on you. Don't waste your energy. You'll need it over the next few years just to get through therapy.

If you dump him

He'll get over it. If, however, he thinks you've slighted him, it's best to watch out for yourself and take extra precautions for the next ten or twenty years. At least.

The Pisces Bastard
FEBRUARY 20–MARCH 20

TO PUT IT MILDLY, PISCES IS A PATHOLOGICAL LIAR.
If you don't believe us, try this little quiz:

> 1. The Pisces bastard you love always looks
> you straight in the eye when he answers a
> slightly tricky question. *True/False*?
> 2. He never tries to avoid answering tricky
> questions whenever humanly possible.
> *True/False*?
> 3. He says he loves you madly and has done
> at least one thing to prove it. *True/False*?

If you answered '*True*' to any of the above you are not
dating a Pisces bastard. Either that or you are a Pisces
bastard, and you're doing this quiz just to prove us right.

Because he's at the arse-end of the zodiac, Pisces is often referred to as the astrological 'rubbish tip'. What this means is he has a little bit of all the other star sign bastards in him, which therefore makes him a bastard twelve times over. This in turn means he's obliged to tell massive fibs so you won't find out the awful truth.

When we first meet someone we like, it's only natural to pretend to be something we're not. Otherwise none of us would ever get a date. However, it's to what extent the truth is stretched that separates the rest of the world from Pisces. For instance, you might be a bus conductor but pretend you actually drive the bus. This is called a 'gross exaggeration'. Pisces, however, will be the bus driver and pretend it's a really interesting job. This is called an 'appalling lie'.

The lies he tells to make himself look better are not to be confused with the little white ones he tells to *protect your feelings* (although how he can confuse his arse with your feelings is a complete mystery to us).

When you accuse him of buying a house with his ex-girlfriend, he will deny it – even though you're holding the deeds embossed with his 'n' her names. Instead he will say the estate agent must have made a typing error. When you look at him in utter disbelief he'll say, okay then, he bought it by accident. When you fall about laughing maniacally, he'll whine that it wasn't his fault – it was yours – and, besides, she made him do it.

But it's the pointless fibs he tells which will really have you reaching for a gun. Pisces will tell you he watched an art-house film when what he really did was sleep through it. He'll say he had a chicken and salad sandwich when he actually had a ham and salad sandwich. Why? Who the hell knows? We're not psychologists. Go ask his.

Fortunately, whilst Pisces was blessed with natural-born cunning and deceit, God denied him long-term vision. So even though he can lie through his teeth to his little heart's content, he won't have the foresight to remember what he said he did, who he said he did it to and why he did it to her in the first place. This means you will *always* find him out.

Obviously, the quicker off the mark you are, the sooner you'll spot the yawning chasm between fact and fiction and the faster you can drop him. Because to be honest, once the initial thrill of catching him out wears off, you'll begin to resent being a full-time lie-detector on legs.

It goes without saying, Pisces only lies when he opens his mouth. This is why he isn't normally very talkative. He figures if he doesn't talk, he can't lie – thus saving you and him a lot of unnecessary grief.

His impressive evasive techniques aren't limited to verbal exchanges, however. He also figures if he avoids you on a physical level, you won't see him for the truly gutless wonder he is.

Unfortunately, this means he'll never be there for you when you actually do have need of him. Don't be upset when he misses the birth of your first child. He'll either have been waylaid because he forgot to put petrol in the car (and petrol is a real and tangible thing whereas he is not), or he's deliberately avoiding it because you might leave him holding the baby.

He's a loser. So why don't you kill him? Well, there's the mandatory life sentence to consider. And there's the community outrage to take into account – after all, everybody loves a Pisces bastard. He's so bloody nice and kind, he makes Mother Teresa want to throw up. Naturally, you end up looking like Lucrezia Borgia on a bad hair day whilst he's busy perfecting his saint *in situ* look.

Truth be known, though, Pisces spends so much time thinking about how caring and sharing he is, he rarely has time to act upon it. That's why he *is* so sweet and tolerant. He never criticises your own foibles because if he does you can do likewise back to him (which you'll do anyway just so you can perpetuate the myth about how he's the Second Coming and you're a complete cow).

Let's be honest here, his passive-aggressive ways could test the patience of Gandhi. The innate ability of Pisces to sit and do and say nothing for years at a time means all decisions are made for him. By you. Which he secretly loves. Especially as most of them are to his detriment (i.e. you leave him) and he's such a consummate martyr. How else can he feel legitimately sorry for himself and get everyone else to do likewise?

'Everyone else' is all his ex-wives and ex-girlfriends, whom he hasn't quite let go of because he hates to get rid of the past. Take the 'pack' out of 'packrat' and it's Pisces. He'll keep some of the Polaroids, most of the love letters and all of the bits of fluff. Real astrologers misconstrue this as his intensely romantic nature. Unless we're missing something here, we're obliged to say it's obviously all inside his head. Don't expect to be deluged with expensive flowers, perfume or engagement rings unless he's just told a whopper and you've just found out. Sweet nothings are all you'll get.

With a straight face and without missing a beat (yes, we've learnt from the best), we can honestly say it's not *surprising* Pisces is known as the zodiac's biggest heartbreaker. Indeed, self-help books abound to help you try to get over him. Here's one for starters:

Lie back in your chair. Take a deep breath and count to ten. You are now feeling calmer – so imagine you're still in love with Pisces . . . Now bloody well wake up.

Excerpt from *Dumping Pathetic Bastards Using Hypnotherapy* © **Lang and Rajah 2004**

How to spot one

Your typical Pisces bastard often has light blue or green eyes. This is God's small way of helping you to spot pupil dilation more easily when he's telling a bald-faced lie. He'll also have small hands and feet – you will later note these are in direct proportion to his spine, brain and everything else that matters.

Where to find one

On a cross feeling sorry for himself. In a Buddhist monastery attempting to stay celibate. At a cosmetic surgery at regular intervals having his nose reduced.

How to intrigue one

Take drugs, screw around and behave badly in public. Then blame it all on your sad, truly pathetic upbringing. This will make him feel better about his own shortcomings whilst at the same time make him want to save you in the vain hope you will look up to him for the rest of your life.

The first date

If you must go anywhere decent, organise it yourself. Otherwise you'll end up walking for miles looking for this really excellent Indian restaurant he's been to and knows is somewhere. Round the corner.

When to do the deed

When he's drunk. When his girlfriend isn't looking. When he feels like it. Don't be surprised when you get had up for date rape in the morning if he regrets what he's done (i.e. if his girlfriend finds out).

When to pop the question

Don't. Whilst your average Pisces bastard quite likes the idea of love ever after, he isn't equipped to deal with harsh realities like showing up at the chapel on time, swearing on the Bible and saying 'I do' when he patently never does.

If he dumps you

He won't, as this would mean he'd have to be responsible for his own actions. Instead he'll engineer it so you have to do it for him – that is, he'll act so unavailable you'll be convinced you aren't going out with him any more so therefore it's okay if you bonk someone else. This affords him the right to be duly devastated and shag all his old flames in an attempt to get on with his life.

If you dump him

You'll play right into his martyr complex. In a cloud of self-denial, he'll start spending quality time with you by following you around in an unmarked car; he'll actually initiate phone calls for the first time ever (but hang up when you answer); and he'll take daring risks for once in his life by appearing at your apartment balcony without use of lift or stairs. The only thing to do is tell him you love him, all is forgiven and you'd like to be the mother of his children. You won't see him for dust. Trust us.

Which bastard are *you* compatible with?

AS EXTENSIVE STUDIES OF THE ZODIAC HAVE shown, star signs can and usually do bring out the worst in the male species (and not just when the bastards are arguing with you about how astrology is a load of old bull).

Unfortunately, unless the convent calls or a crewcut beckons, you're going to have to settle down with one of the bastards eventually. And, anyway, as the saying goes, one woman's meat is another woman's poison – gagging reflexes notwithstanding. In other words, whereas one woman might swoon at a man's planetary pathologies, you might very well pass the bucket. Whereas another woman might go ga-ga over his collective celestial psychoses, you might have to be locked up. And while some women might melt at the sight of his heavenly heathen manners, you'll probably only do so when hell freezes over.

So, go on. Be brave. Find out if you can live with a particular star sign's predictably annoying habits and potentially fatal flaws. Discover if you're destined to love his errant behaviour and wayward ways or if you're more likely to end up being charged for manslaughter. Put yourself at the mercy of the night sky and take the following astro-quizzes, each one carefully designed to show whether or not you'll be able to tolerate the bastard, warts and all.

Be warned, though. We've got a funny feeling that, upon finishing all 12 tests, some of you might well be tempted to don a nun's habit or invest in a really attractive pair of men's dungarees.

Are you compatible with an Aries Bastard?

TAKE THIS TEST AND YOU'LL SEE THAT TO DATE AN Aries bastard is to experience life in a simpler era. A time when men banged rocks together all day long and were still considered valuable members of society. This chest-thumping paradise was otherwise known as the Neolithic Period, which, scientifically speaking, started just after housework was invented and ended well before sensitivity was first discovered in men. Highly evolved, Aries is not. But hirsute, he certainly is.

1. I will date a male only if he is:
   a. A mammal.
   b. A primate.
   c. A large primate.
   d. Capable of speech.

2. There is nothing sexier in a man than:
   a. A full head of hair.
   b. A hairy chest.
   c. A hairy back.
   d. Hairy knuckles.

3. Answer 'True' or 'False'. These things are important to me in a partner:
   a. The ability to use a knife and fork. For eating.
   b. The ability to read a book without pictures.
   c. The ability to dance.
   d. Two eyebrows.

4. Which of the following traits initially attracts you to a man?
   a. A strong smell of sweat.
   b. Spitting.
   c. Chest-beating.
   d. A penis.

5. You are in a bar when two men get into a fight. Do you:
   a. Ignore them.
   b. Feel sexually aroused.
   c. Hope the winner asks you out.
   d. Hope they both ask you out and then start fighting again. Over you.

6. What do you consider to be adequate foreplay?
    a. Any common greeting.
    b. Being shaken awake.
    c. Watching full-contact sport.
    d. None of the above.

7. A fair division of housework between you and your partner is:
    a. You: 100%   Him: None
    b. You: 99%   Him: 1%
    c. You: 98%   Him: 2%
    d. You: 50%   Him: None   The maid: 50%

8. 'Feminism' is:
    a. The belief in and use of labour-saving kitchen appliances (and something you don't subscribe to).
    b. A vaginal deodorant.
    c. A term you are unfamiliar with.
    d. The advocacy of equal rights and opportunities for women.

9. 'Dykes' are women who:
    a. Sometimes forget to shave under their arms.
    b. Refuse to wear push-up bras at all times.
    c. Voice an opinion.
    d. Perform sexual acts with other women for the gratification of heterosexual men.

10. A man offers to help you carry your supermarket bag (holding a loaf of bread and a box of tampons) to your car. You are most likely to:

  a. Perform a sexual favour in return.
  b. Simper gratefully all the way to the car.
  c. Fall instantly, head over heels in love.
  d. Thank him, but say you think you can manage.

HOW TO SCORE

1.	a = 1	b = 2	c = 3	d = 0
2.	a = 1	b = 2	c = 3	d = 4
3.	Score 1 point for every 'False' answer and 0 points for every 'True' answer.			
4.	a = 4	b = 2	c = 3	d = 1
5.	a = 4	b = 2	c = 3	d = −1
6.	a = 4	b = 2	c = 3	d = 0
7.	a = 4	b = 3	c = 2	d = 1
8.	a = 3	b = 4	c = 2	d = −4
9.	a = 3	b = 4	c = 1	d = 2
10.	a = 4	b = 3	c = 4	d = −1

Score less than 0

Congratulations, you two are not of the same species and therefore cannot interbreed.

★THE ARIES BASTARD★

Score between 0 and 10
You are not the sort to get too excited when the Aries bastard beats up other large primates to impress you, but you could still, through tenacity, blind optimism and frequent lapses into stupidity, maintain this relationship for up to twelve months.

Score between 10 and 20
You will have to do all the work in this relationship (especially the housework) but you'll probably be able to put up with Aries long enough to either be out of a job or pregnant. Either way your career will be over but that doesn't matter as it is not as important as his and nowhere near as important as taking care of him.

Score between 20 and 30
Your score reveals a high potential for compatibility with an Aries bastard. We can only hope you're very, very bad at adding up.

Score more than 30
We don't believe you.

Are you compatible with a Taurus Bastard?

TO BE PERFECTLY HONEST, THERE IS NO REAL point in taking this compatibility test. Because, even in the highly likely event that you turn out to be completely unsuited to a Taurus bastard, and then proceed to tell him so, he'll just tell you you're wrong. After all, a typically stubborn Taurean male always knows better than a typically woolly-brained female. Even when he doesn't. And as the zodiac's number-one control freak, he also knows what's good for you. Even though *he* patently isn't.

1. Do you have a mind of your own?
   a. Yes. In fact, I can't believe you are asking me this question.
   b. Er, I think so.
   c. I'm not sure – let me check with my partner.
   d. Baaaaa!

2. Tick the gender stereotype that best applies to you:
   a. I am a typically hysterical and neurotic female.
   b. I am a typically weak and helpless female.
   c. I am a typically impractical and illogical female.
   d. I am a ball-breaking bitch.

3. Tick any of the following tasks you can do without help from a man:
   a. Change my underwear.
   b. Change a light bulb.
   c. Change a flat tyre.
   d. Change my life.

4. I would deem a man too controlling if he:
   a. Refused to let me hold the TV remote.
   b. Refused to let me drive his car.
   c. Refused to let me pay for drinks.
   d. Refused to let me out of the cellar.

5. When it comes to power struggles within relationships, I prefer to:
   a. Encourage them as often as possible.
   b. Not encourage them at all.
   c. Be the first to surrender.
   d. Fight to the death.

6. So far as men in uniforms go, I prefer:
   a. Storm troopers.
   b. Army sergeants.
   c. Naval officers.
   d. Airline stewards.

7. The man I most admire in the entire history of the world is:
   a. Adolf Hitler.
   b. Saddam Hussein.
   c. Genghis Khan.
   d. Mahatma Gandhi.

8. When someone is described as 'a man of huge appetites', you would naturally assume:
   a. He is powerful and exciting.
   b. He is insatiable in bed.
   c. He embraces things with gusto.
   d. He is fat.

9. If a man said he preferred you to take charge in bed, you would think him:
   a. A gentleman.
   b. A pervert.
   c. A liar.
   d. A lazy shit.

10. If you see a man barking orders from the couch in front of the TV, you would instinctively:

    a. Hand him the TV guide.
    b. Hand him a beer.
    c. Hand him his dinner.
    d. Hand him the vacuum cleaner.

HOW TO SCORE

1.	a = –10	b = 1	c = 2	d = 4
2.	a = 4	b = 4	c = 4	d = –10
3.	Score 0 points for ticking a, b and/or c.			
	Score –10 for d.			
4.	a = 2	b = 1	c = –10	d = 4
5.	a = 2	b = 0	c = 4	d = –10
6.	a = 4	b = 2	c = 1	d = –10
7.	a = 4	b = 4	c = 4	d = 0
8.	a = 4	b = 4	c = 4	d = –10
9.	a = 4	b = 0	c = 0	d = –10
10.	a = 1	b = 2	c = 4	d = –10

Score less than 0

Well, a milksop you most certainly are not. And so far as bully-boy tactics go, you're having none of it unless, of course, you're the one barking the orders, threatening merry hell and scaring the bejesus out of men. Truth be told, you've probably got more chance of mating with a eunuch than you have with a Taurus male.

★THE TAURUS BASTARD★

Score between 0 and 10
Sadly for him, you are far too able of body, sound of mind and high of spirit to be truly compatible with a domineering type like Taurus. We strongly suspect you also have a secret aversion to men who are fat, lazy and completely crap in bed.

Score between 10 and 20
Not a *bad* match. Indeed, you might just be the kind of girl to get along with a Taurus bastard – though we use the term 'get along with' rather loosely here as Taurus would be hard-pressed to co-exist peacefully with the Dalai Lama, let alone an occasionally fractious female.

Score between 20 and 30
A Taurus bastard could be just what the doctor ordered (since you clearly haven't listened to your shrink). Pardon us for being so presumptuous, but we're reckoning on the fact that you're probably one of those sickly pale and wan types who would make a consumptive look strong and robust, and have thus had to enlist a Taurus bastard to fill out all your answers to this quiz on your behalf.

Score over 30
Get well soon.

Are you compatible with a Gemini Bastard?

GEMINI BASTARDS ARE COMPLETELY AND UTTERLY mad. They are incapable of holding a thought in their heads for more than a few seconds but can carry on a conversation with an inanimate object for hours. Yet for some unfathomable reason they are allowed to wander freely in society and go on dates with women. So if you've always fancied the village idiot, take this test to see how you'll get on with him.

1. It is important to me that my partner remembers:
   a. My name.
   b. Where he lives.
   c. That he isn't supposed to date other women.
   d. To pick up milk on the way home.

2. My partner tells me he'll be home at 8 p.m. I expect him at:
   a. 8 p.m.
   b. Between 11 p.m. and 1 a.m.
   c. After 3 a.m.
   d. 8 p.m., two days later.

3. I send my partner out for a loaf of bread. I expect him to bring home:
   a. A loaf of bread.
   b. Two Hugo Boss suits, four Armani shirts and a pair of Gucci loafers.
   c. A police escort.
   d. A new girlfriend.

4. Answer 'Yes' or 'No'. I think it's important to be able to trust my partner alone with:
   a. An attractive woman.
   b. A credit card.
   c. Small appliances.
   d. Matches.

5. After several years of marriage, my partner will ideally have:
   a. Established himself in his chosen profession.
   b. Learnt my parents' names.

c. Worn a dress of mine out in public.

d. Permanently misplaced at least one of our children.

6. I would prefer it if my partner's closest friends were:

a. Nice to me.

b. People he's known for longer than a week.

c. Residents of a well-respected mental institution.

d. Imaginary six-foot-tall pink rabbits.

7. You notice an attractive stranger across the room. To get his attention, you:

a. Try to catch his eye, then wait for him to approach you.

b. Trip him up as he walks by.

c. Set fire to your table.

d. Walk over and introduce yourself as the Tooth Fairy.

8. When I read I like to:

a. Sit down.

b. Read a book review and then pretend I've read the book.

c. Colour in the pictures.

d. Lick the pages to check for traps set by mischievous book elves.

9. Which of the following describes your greatest asset in a relationship?
   a. I cope with change well.
   b. I am incredibly forgiving and forgetful.
   c. I am a fully trained psychiatric nurse.
   d. I am generally stupid.

10. I admire a man who feels comfortable in:
   a. His own skin.
   b. A committed relationship.
   c. His birthday suit out in public.
   d. A straitjacket.

HOW TO SCORE

1.	a = 1	b = 1	c = 0	d = 1
2.	a = 0	b = 2	c = 3	d = 4
3.	a = 0	b = 2	c = 3	d = 4
4.	Score 1 point for every 'No' answer and 0 points for every 'Yes' answer.			
5.	a = 0	b = 2	c = 3	d = 4
6.	a = –1	b = 0	c = 3	d = 4
7.	a = 0	b = 2	c = 3	d = 4
8.	a = 1	b = 2	c = 3	d = 4
9.	a = 1	b = 2	c = 3	d = 4
10.	a = 0	b = –1	c = 4	d = 2

★THE GEMINI BASTARD★

Score less than 0
If a Gemini bastard approaches you, hit him with your handbag until he goes away.

Score between 0 and 10
At most you'll enjoy a brief but highly stressful relationship with a Gemini bastard. But whatever you do, don't show him how to turn on your gas stove or you could find yourself homeless and him long gone before you can say: 'Look what you've done, you crazy bastard!'

Score between 10 and 20
If you want this relationship to last, you have to be prepared to make a few sacrifices, as Gemini tends to lose things. But, hopefully, you will learn to live without your life savings, your pets, your children, your faith in humanity and your sense of humour.

Score between 20 and 30
Your score means you are either very compatible with a Gemini bastard or just not terribly bright. Either way you need help.

Score more than 30
You both should be locked up.

Are you compatible with a Cancer Bastard?

IT ACTUALLY DOESN'T MATTER WHETHER YOU'RE compatible with a Cancer bastard. Getting on with him isn't half as important as getting on with the woman who reared him. After all, she's the one responsible for making him the fine figure of a man that he is definitely not today. She's the one he'd invariably thank during acceptance speeches for bravery awards he'll never win (even though he should really be thanking *you* for being charitable enough to *contemplate* dating such a wimp).

1. My definition of a 'mummy's boy' is:
   a. A fully grown man who is kind to his mother.
   b. A fully grown man who still sleeps with his mother.

   c. A fully grown man who knows where his priorities lie.

   d. Probably gay.

2. Tick the statement that best describes your maternal instinct:

   a. I occasionally smile at babies in other people's prams.

   b. I always smile at babies in other people's prams.

   c. I am currently considering stealing babies from other people's prams.

   d. I hate babies of any kind.

3. When it comes to a relationship with a fully grown man, tick the three words that best describe you:

   a. Caring, nurturing, compassionate.

   b. Stoic, patient, long-suffering.

   c. Smothering, overbearing, controlling.

   d. A heartless cow.

4. For me, looking after a fully grown man would include:

   a. Feeding him.

   b. Bathing him.

   c. Wet-nursing him.

   d. None of the above.

5. I believe a fully grown man should, *at least*, be capable of:
    a. Tying his own shoelaces.
    b. Knotting his own tie.
    c. Breathing.
    d. Buying me a drink.

6. For me, a generous gesture from a fully grown man would be:
    a. Expensive jewellery.
    b. Expensive holidays.
    c. A box of peppermint creams.
    d. An occasional smile.

7. When arguing with a fully grown man about his meanness with money, I would prefer that he:
    a. Hurled himself to the floor.
    b. Screamed at the top of his lungs.
    c. Held his breath until he turned blue.
    d. Do 'c' if I could be sure the ambulance couldn't make it on time.

8. When a fully grown man starts crying after I've hacked off the head of his favourite teddy bear, I immediately:
    a. Shudder with embarrassment.
    b. Feel a bit guilty.

   c. Start blubbing too.
   d. Tell him to grow up.

9. Answer 'True' or 'False' to each of the following statements:
   a. It wouldn't bother me if my partner's mother never approved of a single thing I did.
   b. It wouldn't bother me if my partner's mother still gave him pocket money.
   c. It wouldn't bother me if my son continued to live with me after the age of thirty.
   d. It wouldn't bother me if my partner's mother demanded to live with us.

10. Fifty years from now, I would like to be:
   a. Shacked up with my partner in the main house while my partner's mother remained living in the granny flat.
   b. Shacked up in the granny flat while my partner remained living in the main house with his mother.
   c. Shacked up in the main house with my son.
   d. A widow.

HOW TO SCORE

1.	a = 4	b = 2	c = 1	d = 0
2.	a = 1	b = 2	c = 4	d = 0
3.	a = 1	b = 2	c = 4	d = 0
4.	a = 1	b = 2	c = 4	d = 0
5.	a = 0	b = 0	c = 4	d = −10
6.	a = 0	b = 0	c = 0	d = 4
7.	a = 4	b = 4	c = 4	d = 0
8.	a = 1	b = 2	c = 4	d = 0
9.	Score 4 points for every 'True'.			
	Score 0 points for every 'False'.			
10.	a = 2	b = 1	c = 4	d = 0

Score less than 0

Forget it. Babies – big or otherwise – are about as appealing to you as a dose of crabs. And *guess* which star sign has one of those revolting creatures as its symbol?

Score between 0 and 10

Don't even go there. You like men who can stand on their own two feet without the aid of crutches, callipers or corrective shoes.

Score between 10 and 20

Yes, you may have the maternal skills necessary to mollycoddle Cancer. But ask yourself this – is it worth all the sleepless nights? Can you be bothered with all the tears and the tantrums? Do you mind feeling constantly frazzled and woefully inadequate? And that's just the grief you'll get from his goddamned mother.

Score between 20 and 30
You're more than capable of treating a man like a baby. So why not just have a real one instead?

Score over 30
Not that we're for one minute implying that there is anything remiss about these results, but are you, by any chance, a mother? And does your adult son happen to be a Cancer?

Are you compatible with a Leo Bastard?

AS KING OF THE ZODIAC – IF NOT THE WORLD – the Leo bastard is a hard act to follow, not to mention a complete bloody nightmare to date. Indeed, as he himself will tell you at length, this section really should have been entitled 'Are you *good* enough for a Leo bastard?'. But, for the sake of all those female readers out there who have enough insecurities and self-esteem problems as it is, 'compatible' was deemed slightly less undermining and just a tad more realistic.

1. My ideal man would be:
   a. Attractive.
   b. Intelligent.
   c. Good in bed.
   d. One who thinks he is all of the above.

2. The thing I find most repellent in a man is:
   a. Humility.
   b. Modesty.
   c. Selflessness.
   d. None of the above.

3. Before I die, I would like to:
   a. Travel the world.
   b. Discover the meaning of life.
   c. Find a cure for cancer.
   d. Date a man who can't fit his head through the door.

4. The thought of having to constantly flatter a man makes me want to:
   a. Laugh.
   b. Heave.
   c. Kill myself.
   d. Shudder with ecstatic delight.

5. If I were to compliment a man, it would be along the lines of:
   a. 'You make Jude Law look like a complete troll.'
   b. 'Without you, I am nothing.'
   c. 'You *are* the Messiah.'
   d. 'That's a nice shirt.'

6. I would only worship at the altar of a man if:
   a. His name was Jesus.
   b. He paid me a fortune.
   c. I had just had a frontal lobotomy.
   d. He told me to.

7. My definition of a 'dutiful wife' is:
   a. A woman who has given up all hope.
   b. A woman who is a disgrace to the sisterhood.
   c. A woman who knows her place.
   d. A woman who has a self-deluded husband.

8. I would only consider having a child with a man if:
   a. The child was guaranteed to inherit his brains.
   b. The child was guaranteed to inherit his personality.
   c. The child was guaranteed to inherit his looks.
   d. We could adopt.

9. Currently I would rate my self-worth to be:
   a. So high I never wear make-up.
   b. About average (I haven't had an eating disorder yet).
   c. Low enough to make me consider having cosmetic surgery.
   d. So low I generally wear a paper bag over my head.

10. Whenever I attend a large social gathering, I tend to:
   a. Be the life of the party.
   b. Attract admirers.
   c. Mingle easily.
   d. Get mistaken for a pot plant.

HOW TO SCORE

1.	a = 0	b = 0	c = 0	d = 4
2.	a = 4	b = 4	c = 4	d = 0
3.	a = 0	b = 0	c = 0	d = 4
4.	a = 0	b = 0	c = -1	d = 4
5.	a = 1	b = 2	c = 3	d = 0
6.	a = 0	b = 2	c = 1	d = 4
7.	a = 0	b = 0	c = 4	d = 0
8.	a = 4	b = 4	c = 4	d = 0
9.	a = -1	b = 0	c = 1	d = 4
10.	a = 0	b = 0	c = 0	d = 4

Score less than 0

Sorry. You don't stand a chance with Leo. You're far too smart, too confident, too assertive and – worse still – too attractive to be compatible. After all, if there's one thing Leo hates more than anything else in this world, it's competition. Especially from you.

Score between 0 and 10

Again, you think a little too highly of yourself to be a suitable partner for Leo. He likes a woman who's self-effacing, self-deprecating and, above all, extremely grateful for the fact that he doesn't mind being seen out in public with her. Indeed, if you want to appear an attractive proposition, you're going to have to take some pretty drastic measures. So, to affect the appropriate degree of low self-esteem, how about having an industrial accident?

Score between 10 and 20

You certainly have the wavering confidence and the faltering opinions needed to appear remotely enticing to Leo. Simply up the ante on vapid or insipid behaviour and you're sure to catch his eye. For instance, try to dress down even more than you normally do – he won't feel as threatened once you *really* look like something the cat's dragged in. Also, fine-tune your already considerable simpering skills, preferably in front of a mirror (and providing he hasn't got there first). As for expressing any rogue intelligent or independent thoughts in the future? Well, don't. Unless, of course, they come under the guise of compliments to you-know-who.

Score between 20 and 30

You and the Leo bastard are a match made in heaven. He's bright, charismatic, dynamic, personable and . . . well . . . you're not.

Score over 30

Are you *sure* you're not a pot plant?

Are you compatible with a Virgo Bastard?

THE VIRGO BASTARD COMBINES THE VIVACIOUSNESS of a reading lamp and the generosity of Scrooge (pre-ghostly visits) with the social graces of a serial killer. If you're looking for a man no other woman will ever want to steal, you've finally found him. But before you start congratulating yourself, remember, whilst you can take this test to determine your compatibility with a Virgo bastard, *nothing* will prepare you for the tedious and frequently nauseating task of actually dating him.

1. Who, of the following, is your ideal man?
   a. Your tax accountant.
   b. Norman Bates.
   c. Mr Spock.
   d. George Clooney.

2. Your partner is coming to dinner. As part of your seduction routine you might:
   a. Purchase new lingerie.
   b. Put your CD collection in alphabetical order.
   c. Dust off your *Star Trek* video collection.
   d. Clean and disinfect the floors.

3. Sex is:
   a. Great.
   b. For procreation purposes only.
   c. Bearable, as long as it's quick.
   d. Dirty and disgusting.

4. What would you find the most attractive in a man?
   a. The neatly ironed crease in his plaid trousers.
   b. His familiarity with the migrating habits of the Great White Egret.
   c. His meticulous comb-over.
   d. His great sense of humour.

5. One of my personal goals is to:
   a. Attend the Great Texas Birding Classic.
   b. Compare, catalogue and publish all the existing great coin collections (both public and private).
   c. Make a documentary about Rowland Hill, the man responsible for the very first postage stamp.
   d. None of the above.

6. The best document about post office reform by Rowland Hill was called:
   a. *Post Office Reform.*
   b. *Postal Reform.*
   c. Don't know.
   d. Don't care.

7. All the coins in my collection are graded as:
   a. 'Uncirculated' (no marks of wear or damage).
   b. 'Extremely Fine' (no clear signs of wear but finish dulled).
   c. 'Very Fine' (minor wear).
   d. What?

8. I prefer to eat at places which are:
   a. Good value for money.
   b. Cheap.
   c. Very cheap.
   d. Soup kitchens.

9. When the waiter delivers the dinner bill, I would expect my date to:
   a. Offer to take care of it.
   b. Quibble over splitting the bill equally because I had the fish.
   c. Quibble over splitting the bill equally because I ordered a second glass of the house wine.

d. Quibble over splitting the bill equally because I ate more of the complimentary bread.

10. If my partner went to Paris for work, I'd expect to get:
   a. Perfume.
   b. A small plastic replica of the Eiffel Tower.
   c. A postcard (provided postage wasn't too expensive).
   d. Exquisitely small soaps and shampoos with the name of the hotel he stayed in printed on them.

HOW TO SCORE

1.	a = 2	b = 4	c = 4	d = 0
2.	a = −1	b = 2	c = 3	d = 4
3.	a = 0	b = 3	c = 2	d = 4
4.	a = 4	b = 3	c = 2	d = −2
5.	a = 2	b = 4	c = 3	d = 0
6.	a = 10	b = 2	c = 0	d = −2
7.	a = 10	b = 5	c = 4	d = −1
8.	a = 1	b = 2	c = 3	d = 4
9.	a = 0	b = 2	c = 3	d = 4
10.	a = 0	b = 2	c = 3	d = 4

Score less than 0
You just can't see the sexy side of anal retentiveness, can you?

★THE VIRGO BASTARD★

Score between 0 and 10
You have very little in common with a Virgo bastard but if you allow yourself to go on a few dates with him, you'll find you have even less.

Score between 10 and 20
The odds for this relationship working get much better if you don't like sex. But if your brain begins to atrophy from boredom, keep yourself interested by taking on a project together, like comparing, cataloguing and publishing all the existing great coin collections (both public and private). That is, if you really want to.

Score between 20 and 30
A score this high means you are very compatible with a Virgo bastard. It also means you are a boring dweeb.

Score more than 30
We think you will find what you are looking for at the nearest *Star Trek* convention.

Are you compatible with a Libra Bastard?

A LIBRA BASTARD IS NOT MUCH MORE THAN A large Ken doll with movable limbs. He's only appealing to women still under the age of eight. Anyone older will see that he is plastic and empty, with a preference for unrealistically proportioned women. And that because he is completely shallow, he lacks the depth required to make a decision or a commitment. The Libra bastard will never make either. So even if you find compatibility in this test, be warned: Libra, like Ken, hasn't the balls required to make a relationship work.

1. You are at a restaurant and you have to decide between the green salad and the lasagne. Which do you choose to eat?
   a. The salad.
   b. The lasagne.

   c. Both.
   d. Neither.

2. My favourite colour is:
   a. Blue.
   b. Red. No, blue. No, red. Or green . . .
   c. I don't know.
   d. I do know but it isn't listed here.

3. Which of the following traits is most important to you in a partner?
   a. The ability to decide which socks to wear with which outfits.
   b. The ability to use shampoo and conditioner in the right order.
   c. The ability to use women.
   d. Genitals that are visible to the naked eye.

4. To make my partner happy I would consider giving up:
   a. Smoking.
   b. Drinking.
   c. Eating.
   d. Thinking.

5. After five years of marriage, I would expect my husband to:
   a. Remember our anniversary.
   b. Hire a gorgeous young secretary in a short skirt.
   c. Leave me for his gorgeous young secretary.
   d. Leave his gorgeous young secretary for the receptionist.

6. In a secure relationship I expect my partner to:
   a. Encourage me.
   b. Encourage me to use wrinkle cream.
   c. Encourage me to improve myself with plastic surgery.
   d. Encourage my eating disorder.

7. Which of the following job titles most resembles your own?
   a. Miss Venezuela.
   b. Miss July.
   c. Doctor Barbie.
   d. (gorgeous young) Secretary (in a short skirt).

8. How old are you?
   a. Sixteen.
   b. Over twenty-five (but very, very, very beautiful and/or very, very, very rich and/or very, very, very famous).

c. Seventeen.
d. None of the above.

9. What is your body type?
a. Average.
b. Tall and very thin with big breasts.
c. Short and very thin with big breasts.
d. Medium height and very thin with big breasts.

10. Answer 'Yes' or 'No'. Do you possess any of the following?
a. The phone number of a very talented plastic surgeon.
b. A lot of time on your hands.
c. A desire not to get married in this lifetime.
d. Your own, best-selling, swimsuit calendar.

HOW TO SCORE

1.	a = 3	b = 0	c = −1	d = 4
2.	a = 2	b = 3	c = 4	d = 0
3.	a = 2	b = 3	c = 4	d = −2
4.	a = 1	b = 2	c = 3	d = 4
5.	a = −1	b = 2	c = 3	d = 4
6.	a = 0	b = 2	c = 3	d = 4
7.	a = 4	b = 3	c = 2	d = 1
8.	a = 4	b = 3	c = 2	d = 0
9.	a = −1	b = 4	c = 3	d = 2
10.	Score 2 points for every 'Yes' answer and 0 points for every 'No' answer.			

★THE LIBRA BASTARD★

Score less than 0
You would rather date a lamp-post.

Score between 0 and 10
Any score over zero means that at some point you're likely to sleep with a Libra bastard and then regret that you did for the rest of your life.

Score between 10 and 20
You have a good chance with a Libra bastard. If you play your cards right and are willing to wait a decade or so, you could end up being the woman he settles for once all his other options have fizzled out. But don't hold your breath.

Score between 20 and 30
Once you're oh-so-happy and completely secure in this relationship the Libra bastard will leave you for no apparent reason. At first you won't understand it, but sooner or later you'll discover the 'no apparent reason' was a girl at least five years younger than you.

Score more than 30
You are the perfect match for a Libra bastard but this in no way guarantees he won't leave you for someone better looking.

Are you compatible with a Scorpio Bastard?

ANY RELATIONSHIP OF ANY LENGTH WITH A Scorpio bastard is guaranteed to wreck your emotional health, your self-esteem or, at the very least, your enjoyment of life. He is a sneaky, nasty, controlling bastard, a master manipulator and a world-class pervert. But, his good points aside, there are also many reasons to avoid him. So take this test before you find yourself involved with Scorpio and chasing three valium with a bottle of vodka just to get to sleep every night.

1. I have the following in my wardrobe:
   a. At least one of these items: stiletto heels; fishnet stockings; black underwear; a suspender belt; a corset; a short black leather skirt; crotchless panties; something see-through; handcuffs; or a push-up bra.

   b. A nun's habit.

   c. My old school uniform.

   d. My current school uniform.

2. How would you rate your sexual prowess?
   a. Unbelievable, and I have the professionally shot videos to prove it (you can also check me out on my website: www.wet'n'wild.com).
   b. Actually, I'm still a virgin.
   c. I'm incredible, and I charge accordingly.
   d. None of the above.

3. Who of the following comes closest to your ideal man?
   a. Count Dracula.
   b. Marquis de Sade.
   c. Svengali.
   d. None of the above.

4. Of the following, my favourite book is:
   a. *Lolita* – Vladimir Nabokov.
   b. *Interview with a Vampire* – Anne Rice.
   c. *120 Days of Sodom* – Marquis de Sade.
   d. *Alice in Wonderland* – Lewis Carroll.

5. Obsession is:
    a. A natural progression of feelings in a relationship.
    b. Highly underrated.
    c. A perfume by Calvin Klein.
    d. A necessary part of any co-dependent, sado-masochistic union.

6. Which of the following group activities most appeals to you?
    a. An Alcoholics Anonymous meeting.
    b. Group therapy.
    c. Basketball.
    d. A *ménage a trois*.

7. I think it's perfectly normal and acceptable that my boyfriend has:
    a. Had more sexual experience than me.
    b. Stayed out all night with no explanation as to his whereabouts.
    c. Tried to sleep with every woman he has ever met.
    d. Two or three ex-girlfriends who've tried to commit suicide.

8. Generally speaking your life so far has been:
    a. Charmed.
    b. Dogged by inequality and injustice.
    c. One tragic mistake after another.
    d. Not worth living.

9. Answer 'True' or 'False'. When I get married, it is important to me that I keep:
   a. My name.
   b. My sense of humour.
   c. My sanity.
   d. My husband.

10. The best way to end a relationship is to:
   a. Walk away.
   b. Overdose.
   c. Shoot my partner, his mistress and myself.
   d. Check into a psychiatric institution.

HOW TO SCORE

1.	a = 1	b = 2	c = 3	d = 4
2.	a = 4	b = 10	c = 3	d = 0
3.	a = 2	b = 4	c = 3	d = 1
4.	a = 2	b = 3	c = 4	d = 1
5.	a = 4	b = 3	c = 0	d = 2
6.	a = 3	b = 2	c = 0	d = 4
7.	a = 1	b = 2	c = 3	d = 4
8.	a = 0	b = 1	c = 3	d = 4
9.	Score 1 point for every 'False' answer and 0 points for every 'True' answer.			
10.	a = 0	b = 3	c = 2	d = 4

★THE SCORPIO BASTARD★

Score less than 0

There's not a hope in hell of this relationship ever getting off the ground but the Scorpio bastard will want to sleep with you anyway.

Score between 0 and 10

Any time spent with a Scorpio will make you truly appreciate the time you don't spend with him.

Score between 10 and 20

Be very afraid. You won't be able to prevent Scorpio from doing exactly what he wants to do to whomever he wants to do it to. This relationship will end with you in full-time psychiatric care or featured in a shocking, lead story of 'love, betrayal and murder' on the six o'clock news. They will probably also make a TV movie about you.

Score between 20 and 30

You are very compatible with Scorpio but even if you really do enjoy keeping abreast of the latest trends in sexual perversion it won't change the fact that you are in a relationship with a sadistic bastard and you won't have any fun.

Score more than 30

Oh dear.

Are you compatible with a Sagittarius Bastard?

BLESSED WITH THE SMARTS OF A PARTICULARLY backward brontosaurus and the sort of sexual appetite that even Caligula would deem excessive, the Sagittarius bastard is compatible with very few women. Not because he's fussy – he's not. It's just that most women prefer a man who thinks with his brain. The following questions should determine whether you're one of the clueless few who would stoop to dating him. (Of course, if you are, you're possibly not smart enough to actually complete this test.)

1. My IQ is:
   a. High enough to gain me admittance to Mensa.
   b. High enough to hold down a regular job.
   c. High enough to recognise an idiot when I see one.
   d. 80.

2. I am too smart to consider dating:
   a. A man who is rich and successful.
   b. A man who is capable of being faithful.
   c. A man who is sharp and witty.
   d. A moron.

3. I can tell a man is intelligent by the fact that he:
   a. Breathes.
   b. Walks.
   c. Talks.
   d. Asks me out.

4. My partner's sexual history is:
   a. Irrelevant – even if he has slept with a thousand females.
   b. Important – especially if he has slept with a thousand females.
   c. Necessary to know only if one of those females was a barnyard animal.
   d. Necessary to know only if the barnyard animal was underage.

5. In which situations should your partner *know* when to be tactful (tick where applicable):
   a. When I ask him whether the barnyard animal was prettier than me.
   b. When I ask him if the barnyard animal was slimmer than me.

   c. When I ask him if the barnyard animal was better in bed than me.

   d. When I ask him if he's ever felt tempted to sleep with my sister.

6. Should my partner be dumb enough to admit that he was sleeping with my sister, I would forgive him if:

   a. I was sleeping with his brother.

   b. My sister had cloven hooves.

   c. He was dumb enough to believe that I could forgive him.

   d. He died tragically in the process.

7. Should my partner love me and leave me in an insultingly short period of time, I would:

   a. Think him a brain-dead fool.

   b. Wonder if I've caught something nasty from him.

   c. Shrug and think, 'Oh well, if you love someone, you should set him free . . .'

   d. Hunt him down and kill him.

8. My definition of a 'commitment-phobe' is:

   a. A man who ejaculates within twenty-five seconds.

   b. A man who dumps his girlfriend within twenty-five days.

   c. A man who leaves his wife within twenty-five years.

   d. A man.

9. Sexual promiscuity aside, tick which habitual behaviour you would be unable to tolerate in a man:
   a. Gambling.
   b. Gambling.
   c. Gambling.
   d. All of the above.

10. If I found out that my partner had stupidly gambled all our life savings on the horses, I would:
   a. Shoot him (my partner, that is, not the horse).
   b. Roll my eyes and whinny a lot.
   c. Have a bit of a chuckle – after all, it is only money for our retirement.
   d. Find that hard to believe since I had already squandered the money on the horses the day before.

HOW TO SCORE

1.	a = 0	b = 1	c = 2	d = 3
2.	a = -3	b = -3	c = -3	d = 3
3.	a = 3	b = 3	c = 3	d = 0
4.	a = 3	b = 0	c = 1	d = 2
5.	a = 0	b = 0	c = 0	d = 0
6.	a = 3	b = 2	c = 1	d = 0
7.	a = 0	b = 0	c = 3	d = 0
8.	a = 3	b = 2	c = 1	d = 0
9.	a = 0	b = 0	c = 0	d = –10
10.	a = 0	b = 1	c = 2	d = 3

Score less than 0

This is possibly the one and only time in your life when being an intelligent woman is a blessing rather than a curse . . . you are way too smart to ever end up with a Sagittarius bastard.

Score between 0 and 10

The only way you could possibly find any common ground with a Sagittarius bastard is by first wilfully ramming your head into a brick wall. Repeatedly. Until unconsciousness sets in.

Score between 10 and 20

The Sagittarius bastard isn't your best match by a long shot. To avoid any potential communication breakdowns, try speaking with your tongue hanging out of your mouth. And to keep his out-of-control libido and spending habits in check, always carry a large kitchen knife.

Score between 20 and 30

So far as physical attraction goes, you two are on the same wavelength. Sex is obviously extremely important to both of you, though not necessarily just sex with each other. Sadly, there won't be any meeting of the minds – mainly because neither of you actually have one.

Score over 30

Hah! Tricked you! The highest score possible for this compatibility test is 24. In other words, you're as thick as he is.

Are you compatible with a Capricorn Bastard?

WE WERE GOING TO DITCH THIS PARTICULAR TEST completely since, so far as your being suited to a humourless drone like a Capricorn bastard is concerned, star signs have got absolutely nothing to do with it. The dollar signs in your eyes and on your bank statements are the only things that really count. Not very romantic, we know. But what else do you expect from the one man in the zodiac who thinks the planet Mars was named after a global megacorp and always laughs uproariously whenever you mention Uranus?

1. Money is:
    a. Not everything.
    b. A means to an end.
    c. The source of all evil.
    d. My entire *raison d'être*.

2. If I absolutely *had* to sell my own grandmother, I would only do so on the proviso that:
   a. I got a really good price for her.
   b. I did not have to pay any capital gains tax afterwards.
   c. The buyer was willing to take grandfather as well.
   d. This is a hypothetical question only.

3. When I see a scruffy old tramp, I:
   a. Recoil in horror at the injustices in this world.
   b. Recoil in horror at his taste in clothes.
   c. Think there but for the grace of God go I in my new Gucci dress.
   d. Not applicable – I refuse to make eye contact with plebs.

4. I would only fail to show up for dinner at Buckingham Palace if:
   a. I wasn't invited.
   b. I was an avid anti-royalist.
   c. I couldn't get an appointment with my hair salon beforehand.
   d. I got a better offer (like, say, an invitation to the White House).

5. If I were to marry a man with abbreviations after his name, it would have to be:
   a. CEO.
   b. HRH.
   c. PhD.
   d. DSS.

6. How important is sex in a relationship?
   a. More important than a weekly pedicure but less important than a weekly manicure.
   b. More important than a weekly manicure but less important than a weekly facial.
   c. Equally as important as a weekly facial.
   d. None of the above.

7. Tick any of the following that you find even faintly amusing:
   a. Tax Code 12b – Section iii.
   b. Fart cushions.
   c. The G8 Summit.
   d. The jokes found inside Christmas crackers.

8. What would initially attract you to a very rich man?
   a. His charm.
   b. His wit.
   c. His personality.
   d. His money.

9. If you were married to a very rich man, you would resent any of his money going to (tick where applicable):
   a. Social welfare.
   b. His mistress.
   c. Poor relatives.
   d. His secret offshore bank account.

10. If, while married, your very rich husband was facing financial difficulties, which of the following would you sacrifice?
   a. My personal chef.
   b. My cleaning lady.
   c. My sex therapist.
   d. My husband – because then I figure I wouldn't need any of the above.

HOW TO SCORE

1.	a = 1	b = 2	c = -1	d = 4
2.	a = 1	b = 2	c = 4	d = -1
3.	a = 0	b = 1	c = 2	d = 4
4.	a = 1	b = 0	c = 2	d = 4
5.	a = 2	b = 4	c = 1	d = -1
6.	a = 4	b = 2	c = 1	d = -1
7.	Score 4 points for each answer ticked.			
8.	a = 0	b = -10	c = 0	d = 4
9.	Score 4 points for each answer ticked.			
10.	a = 4	b = 4	c = 4	d = 0

Score less than 0

Unfortunately, due to your high moral standards and strong social conscience, you are the sort of girl who would never sleep with *any* man for a million bucks, let alone a Capricorn.

Score between 0 and 10

You and a Capricorn bastard will probably never get it together – mainly because you share no common interests or hobbies like making money, collecting dosh or creating dough.

Score between 10 and 20

You are definitely a material girl and will no doubt enjoy being able to shop until your hard-working, over-achieving Capricorn bastard drops dead of a heart attack. However, you could find that an abundance of material possessions in no way compensates for the fact that he's a boring old git who's about as much fun to be around as a corpse with chronic depression.

Score between 20 and 30

You are clearly as craven, capitalistic and as social-climbing as he is, so the two of you could be the perfect pair. A little word of advice, though. Do not sign any prenups. That way, you can take him for squillions when you eventually come to your senses and demand a divorce.

Score over 30

You deserve all the money – and the resulting long-term marital misery – you will get.

Are you compatible with an Aquarius Bastard?

ON FIRST APPEARANCES, HE SEEMS LIKE ANY normal bloke. However, as this compatibility test should quickly prove, the Aquarius bastard is about as 'normal' as a pig with wings. While other men might be from Mars, Aquarius flies in another galaxy entirely. This, in turn, could lead you to think he is actually more morally superior and ethically sound than the rest of his male peers. Don't be fooled. It makes him different to the other eleven bastards, not *better*.

1. My idea of being politically correct is:
   a. Refusing to tell man-bashing jokes.
   b. Refusing to laugh at man-bashing jokes.
   c. Refusing to read books full of man-bashing jokes.
   d. Knowing how to spell the word 'politician'.

2. The social issue that concerns me most at the moment is:
   a. Dwarf throwing.
   b. Foot binding.
   c. Parrot smuggling.
   d. What to wear on my next hot date.

3. Answer either 'True' or 'False' to each of the following statements:
   a. I often picket venues that host cock-fighting competitions.
   b. I have sabotaged at least one vehicle that transports nuclear warheads.
   c. In my spare time, I usually plant crops for farms in poverty-stricken countries.
   d. Just recently, I freed two rats and nine rabbits from a medical laboratory.

4. When was the last time you tried to 'make a difference'?
   a. The time just before I won the Nobel Peace Prize.
   b. The time just after I discovered the Missing Link.
   c. The time during World War II when I joined the Resistance.
   d. None of the above.

5. The books most likely to be found on my bookshelf are written by:
   a. Descartes, Socrates and Sartre.
   b. Germaine Greer, Gloria Steinem and Naomi Wolf.
   c. Jung, Freud and Nietzsche.
   d. J.K. Rowling.

6. A man in touch with his feminine side is:
   a. A contradiction in terms.
   b. A pain in the arse.
   c. A closet homosexual.
   d. All of the above.

7. Should a man *not* try to maul me on our first date together, I would be:
   a. Flattered.
   b. Mortified.
   c. Concerned about his sexual orientation.
   d. Tempted to make a lunge at him.

8. I would only consider having a platonic relationship with a man if:
   a. I didn't fancy him.
   b. I was a lesbian.
   c. He was directly related to me.
   d. He insisted that sex was a base and brutal ritual

devised by male pornographers to demean, devalue and dehumanise women.

9. Choose the statements which best represent your philosophies on marriage:
   a. Marriage is a very special symbol of love and commitment between a man and a woman.
   b. Marriage is a misogynistic institution designed by men to oppress and enslave the female masses.
   c. Marriage is a concept created by evil pharmaceutical companies to encourage women to buy more anti-depressants.
   d. Marriage is a government conspiracy designed to clamp down on single mothers' benefits.

10. If you absolutely had to, you would sleep with:
   a. A chauvinist pig.
   b. A capitalist pig.
   c. A farmyard pig.
   d. A self-righteous prig.

HOW TO SCORE

1.	a = 4	b = 4	c = 4	d = 0
2.	a = 4	b = 4	c = 4	d = 0
3.	Score 4 points for every 'True' and 0 points for every 'False'.			
4.	a = 4	b = 4	c = 4	d = 0

5.	a = 4	b = 4	c = 4	d = −10
6.	a = 0	b = 0	c = 0	d = −1
7.	a = 4	b = 0	c = 0	d = −1
8.	a = 0	b = 0	c = 0	d = 4
9.	a = 0	b = 4	c = 4	d = 4
10.	a = 0	b = 0	c = 0	d = 4

Score less than 0

For a frivolous sort such as yourself, dating a right-on, right-pain-in-the-posterior Aquarius bastard would be about as much fun as eating a wet blanket. At gunpoint. On a dark night. Halfway up the Congo.

Score between 0 and 10

Though your heart is in the right place, you possibly do not have the ethical commitment nor the strong moral fibre (not to mention the appropriate footwear) to stand alongside Aquarius, knee-deep in mud in some godforsaken swamp, campaigning against the near-extinction of some animal you've never heard of because you don't subscribe to *National Geographic*.

Score between 10 and 20

You're obviously up on hot political issues and a dab hand at philosophical debate. Things could go horribly pear-shaped, however, should you slack off occasionally and demand he indulge in something less intellectually challenging – like sex, for instance.

Score between 20 and 30
Brilliant. You and Aquarius were made for each other. Now can you please remove him from the dating scene, thus saving the rest of us from having to listen to him constantly banging on about the plight of African pygmies . . . on the first *date*.

Score over 30
You seriously need to lighten up.

Are you compatible with a Pisces Bastard?

THE PISCES BASTARD IS SO CHRONICALLY unfaithful, so compulsively dishonest and so patently destined for failure that there should be no need for this compatibility test. No sane woman would want him (and that includes his current wife). But, in truth, every woman (including his wife) should take this test. It doesn't matter who you *think* you're dating (or who you *think* you're married to), he could be a Pisces bastard trying to look more attractive by passing himself off as another star sign.

1. Honesty is:
   a. Highly overrated.
   b. Unromantic.
   c. A quaint, outdated notion.
   d. Essential to a relationship.

2. Answer 'Yes' or 'No'. It would upset you if you phoned your partner and:
   a. He pretended to be his answering machine.
   b. He faked an accent and said you had the wrong number.
   c. His wife answered the phone.
   d. He had given you the number of his dentist.

3. Which 'little white lie' is acceptable from a partner?
   a. 'No.' (In answer to: 'Do I look fat?')
   b. 'My wife doesn't understand me.'
   c. 'I'm thirty-fifth in line for succession to the throne of England.'
   d. 'I'm not really married to her any more.'

4. I'd like my partner to be:
   a. A lying, two-timing sleazebag.
   b. A pathetic, no-account loser.
   c. A disgrace to the human race.
   d. None of the above.

5. Love is:
   a. A lie.
   b. A series of lies.
   c. Never having to say you're sorry, no matter who you just slept with.
   d. None of the above.

6. Your partner tells you he doesn't deserve you. You:
   a. Assume this means he loves you.
   b. Assume he's too good for you.
   c. Assume he's having an affair.
   d. Believe him.

7. You see your partner kissing an attractive blonde, but when questioned he denies the incident. You:
   a. Believe him when he says he was resuscitating a poor buxom girl who'd fainted.
   b. Get your eyesight checked.
   c. Don't know what to believe.
   d. Knee him in the balls.

8. Your partner tells you he wants to see other people. You:
   a. Point out that the three affairs he has had count as 'seeing other people'.
   b. Say that is fine, but he has to leave his wife first.
   c. Tell him he can see other people so long as they are therapists.
   d. Knee him in the balls.

9. To make up for being unfaithful, I would expect my partner to:
   a. Buy me a punnet of strawberries.
   b. Read me a badly written sonnet.

c. Behave with the utmost integrity, loyalty and fidelity in the future.
d. Take a knee in the balls.

10. When I get married I'd prefer:
a. A big, old-fashioned white wedding.
b. That the bridesmaids did not sleep with the groom.
c. The groom to be present at the ceremony.
d. To elope so the groom's current wife doesn't find out.

HOW TO SCORE

1.	a = 3	b = 4	c = 2	d = –2
2.	Score 2 points for every 'No' answer and 0 points for every 'Yes' answer.			
3.	a = 1	b = 2	c = 4	d = 3
4.	a = 10	b = 10	c = 10	d = 0
5.	a = 3	b = 4	c = 2	d = 0
6.	a = 4	b = 3	c = 0	d = –1
7.	a = 3	b = 4	c = 2	d = 0
8.	a = 4	b = 4	c = 1	d = 0
9.	a = 4	b = 3	c = –10	d = 1
10.	a = 3	b = 0	c = 0	d = 4

★THE PISCES BASTARD★

Score less than 0
Due to his Piscean intuition, he'll know you know he's a pathetic loser and will hopefully stay away.

Score between 0 and 10
You will allow the Pisces bastard into your life just long enough for his lies to really, really annoy you.

Score between 10 and 20
You are compatible with a Pisces bastard, and if you can wait for him to leave his wife or girlfriend for you, then you'll give him the time and opportunity he needs to cheat on you too.

Score between 20 and 30
You will end up married to a Pisces bastard, as wife number one, two, three, four or five. The marriage will last only if he (through no fault of his own) has a lot of money and doesn't want you to get half.

Score more than 30
You deserve him. Sorry.